THE FEMININE HERBAL BEAUTY

Learn to grow, make, use and preserve your own beauty herbs.

INTRODUCTION

Beauty is a weapon, knowledge is a force, and compassion is preservation. Sad to say, but for women, beauty and strength go hand in hand. Whether you like it or not, women's power does, in fact, some places depend on how they appear. Don't get me wrong, intelligence is certainly lovely, but our culture also places a high importance on physical attractiveness. Because everyone has a different definition of beauty, the topic of beauty is challenging. That much is certain. Beauty can, however, be used as a weapon of advantage.

Nature is the interaction of our physical environment with the life that exists there, including the atmosphere, climate, natural resources, ecosystem, flora, animals, and people. Nature is the earth's most priceless gift from God. It is the main source of all the things that all living things on Earth need to survive. Nature provides everything we need, including the food we eat, the clothing we wear, and the home we live in. Nature is referred to as "Mother Nature" because, like our mother, she is constantly taking care of all of our needs.

From the minute we leave our house, everything we see is a product of nature. Everything that contributes to our environment's beauty and allure, including the trees, flowers, landscapes, insects, sunlight, and breeze, is a product of nature. In a nutshell, nature is our habitat. Even before the evolution of humans, nature existed.

Mankind is a vital and integral aspect of nature. It is one of life's greatest blessings, but modern humans no longer acknowledge it as such. Many poets, writers, artists, and others have drawn ideas and sources from nature over the years. They were motivated by this amazing creation to write stories and poetry about it. They had genuinely shown an appreciation for nature, and it was evident in their work even now. Nature is essentially everything that surrounds us, including the air we breathe, the water we drink, the sun we enjoy, the birds we hear chirping, the moon we see, and more. It contains both living and non-living objects. Therefore, modern people should take a cue from their forebears and begin appreciating nature before it's too late.

Importance of nature

Nature existed long before humans did, and ever since, it has looked after and sustained humanity. In other words, it provides us with a shield that protects us from all injuries and damage. Humanity must realize that it is impossible to survive without nature.

Even if nature can defend us, it also has the capability to destroy humanity. Nature in all its forms, including plants, animals, rivers, mountains, the moon, and more, is equally important to us. One component alone can have a destructive effect on how human life operates.

By consuming foods and beverages that are naturally healthy, we can live a healthy lifestyle. In a similar way, it gives us food and water so we can function. The two essential components for survival—rainfall and sunshine—come directly from nature.

Additionally, only nature can give us the oxygen we breathe and the wood we utilize for a variety of functions. But as technology advances, fewer people are observing the natural world. The need to balance and conserve natural resources is becoming more and more urgent, necessitating prompt action.

Growing up in an extended family of four generations in the countryside of a small town in Essex, I observed the close relationship between my nana and the plants. She had a deep appreciation for nature, and gardening was her favorite pastime. Every herb and shrub I can think of was planted by her, and she used 7 different species. "Everything seven represents for perfection," she said, "and a union of seven will reproduce good fortune." Every Sunday we would bathe in a mixture of goat milk, lavender, and white and red roses as part of a ritual. Fresh spices and veggies from her garden were used to create every meal. She used her formulations to cure all common illnesses, and she is knowledgeable about which herbs work best for which conditions. She was a veritable encyclopedia of information about herbs, and she made care to instill in us a love of nature and a habit of gardening.

From ancient times to the present, the knowledge of plants has been passed down. Herbs are a powerful source of healing and are essential to the body's upkeep. However, there are also lethal and poisonous herbs that can hurt humans, just like there are two sides to every coin. Therefore, before doing anything, it is necessary to have a basic understanding of herbs and bushes.

Although this is a generality, the majorities of herbs produce seeds, lack a woody stem, and wither away to the ground in the winter. However, many other plants that we don't typically think of as herbs also do. Rather than what they are, plants are called "herbs" because of what they are used for. Herbs are plants that are either utilized as food flavoring, fragrance, or medication. Typically, culinary herbs only employ the leaves or seeds, whereas medicinal and cosmetic herbs use all parts of the plant (flowers, leaves, stem, and root). We do, however, employ Horse Chestnut seeds (conkers) and Ginkgo leaves as herbs in our products to highlight specific exceptions that prove the rule. In essence, herbs are plants that provide advantages. Herbs have been applied to the skin for hundreds of years; as kids, we were all taught that dock leaves eased stinging nettle rash itching. As we expanded, we used this understanding and centuries of conventional wisdom to create products that condition and improve skin health, ease discomfort, and lessen irritation. Herbs are also very beneficial for sensitive skin because they are made from natural, organic substances. You may find rows of skincare items with plant-based ingredients at any beauty counter. Pomegranate seed oil regenerating creams, ginseng root anti-wrinkle serums, and kelp extract-infused face masks are other examples. In the world of high-end beauty, there are two signals at work. The first is that plants can heal us from the outside in. The other, more subtle message is conveyed by the aura of mystery surrounding botanical extracts. Even while many of the extracts you may encounter seem strange, many others become more accessible. At the grocery store or farmers' market, you can get them fresh or dried. They might even flourish in your garden, either on purpose or as 'weeds'. Thyme, which fights acne, aloe Vera, which is calming, and rose petals, which are gently toning, are just a few of the ingredients.

Advantages of Natural Skincare

Inner beauty blossoms: This well-known saying is accurate on many levels, but I'd want to focus on the skin-related one. Thyme, rosemary, sage, and calendula are just a few of the many herbs used for skin care that are both edible and frequently used in food. Furthermore, their use both inside and outside is crucial for healthy skin, which makes them safe to employ in homemade beauty remedies. A bad diet has a negative impact on our energy levels, emotions, and how our skin feels, looks, and functions. Here are some advantages of using herbal cosmetics:

The Touch of Mother Nature: Herbal products are entirely based on what Nature produces and provides to us. The goods are produced using natural materials in a secure and safe way. It has so far reached out to those who think that herbs have great healing powers and can make them feel as natural as possible. You'll experience living among the natural world when Mother Nature touches you. The products don't use any animal products because they are manufactured with natural ingredients. Therefore, using herbal products is essential if you want to attain completely natural and perfect skin because they are created without the use of synthetic ingredients

Skin-safe: As previously discussed, natural herbal remedies are described as being skin-safe. Regarding safety, these products are totally secure. In contrast to other goods that could include a small percentage of chemical bases, their application is completely safe and they have no negative effects. The use of herbal products is the key to having beautiful, healthy skin as you age. Because they are manufactured from botanical ingredients that are loaded with natural vitamins and antioxidants, they are gentle on the skin. With time, they can only help your skin become soft and healthy.

Good for all skin types: All skin types can use herbal products. Your skin deserves to occasionally be given some tender loving care, whether it is sensitive, oily, or mixed skin. Due to the fact that they are entirely herbal and have no side effects, these herbal solutions are ideal for all skin types. All you have to do is concentrate on your skin type and the substance that must be appropriate for you! These products take care of all skin problems and relieve any skin tension.

Natural fragrance: As a user, it's critical to feel the products you use. One of the most crucial components for treating your skin from the inside out is the smell. Such products' fragrances and aromas quiet your mind as well as your skin by relaxing both. These items are recommended for use because they are absolutely free of any synthetic or harmful odors. You may experience severe headaches and skin reactions from certain strong odors. Products created from organic herbs and plants retain the inherent flavor of the component. Natural items are naturally scented because they don't include any artificial smell.

No internal harm: Of all the key advantages of utilizing herbal skin care products, this is the one that will increase your trust in them because it prevents any inside damage to your skin. These products' principal function is to deeply cleanse the skin without causing injury. These are entirely safe for you because your skin isn't supplied with artificial nutrients or pollutants. Your skin will effectively recover, however it can take some time.

Growing your own herbs for skincare can benefit both your health and beauty regimen. Being outside and near plants alone can lengthen your life. Your wellbeing is influenced by the light exercise, vitamin D from sunlight, and effect on mood. I can personally attest to this.

Cosmetics terminology

• Balm- A firm oil-based product called a balm needs to be massaged into the skin. A small bit of beeswax, soy wax, or hard oil provides the hardness.

• Salve - Much softer than balms, salves are another option. Compared to balms, they have a larger concentration of liquid oils.

•Lotion- There are two different types of lotion. Skin-cleansing products include either a thin cream or a herbal water infusion.

• Cream - Using an emulsifier, you can create creams by combining a tiny amount of oil with a lot of water.

• Decoction - You can make a concentrated liquid by heating or boiling difficult plant material, like roots and bark, in water.

• Oil infusion- The infusion of dried plant material into a carrier oil.

•Water infusion- Fresh or dried plant material is infused into water, typically distilled, to create a water infusion. Basically a tea

• Rinse- This is an infusion of water that you apply to your skin or hair. The botanical extracts remain after the water content has evaporated during the drying process.

•Serum-Concentrated plant extracts in liquid oil or water are found in serum. After cleaning your skin, but before moisturizing, you apply it.

•Tincture- This is a type of alcohol infusion that typically contains dried (or low water content) plant material. Additionally, you can infuse it with glycerin to create a tincture.

• Toner is a liquid that you use cotton wool to apply to your skin. Some astringent substances can tighten skin and eliminate grease. Others are kinder and help with cleaning and renewing.

Chapter 1

Herbs, plants, and flowers for skincare

There are countless plants that you can use to create your own arsenal of cosmetic products. Others hydrate, while yet others treat acne. Some are excellent at relaxing sensitive skin. Many plants have numerous skincare benefits and can be utilized to treat a variety of skin issues. One of my favorite plants, calendula, may be used to treat a variety of conditions, including eczema, burns, wounds, acne, and more. Your skin may become damaged for a variety of reasons. Just a handful includes injuries, bruises, drugs or medical treatment, burns or sunburn. When treating damaged skin, stick to mild rinses, salves, and creams that promote skin regeneration and protection.

Herbs for Skincare that Heals

Calendula (Calendula Officinalis)

This flower's golden petals contain extracts that calm the skin, lessen swelling, and treat burns, sunburns, acne, eczema, and skin abrasions. Use the extraction technique of water or oil infusion. Salves, balms, creams, lotions, toners, and rinses are examples of possible applications. Calendula can also be used to prepare a tincture that you can apply topically to acne. Calendula officinalis, one of the most popular and easy-to-grow medicinal herbs, is not only simple to cultivate but also a potent and effective skincare herb. Its blossoms are mild astringents and wash the skin, alleviate cold sores and chapped lips, disinfect minor wounds, hasten healing, and speed up healing. Calendula officinalis is a bright garden plant that has flowers that range in color from yellow to orange and can bloom all year long. In addition, because they are edible, medicinal, and decorative, they are possibly the most practical garden flower you can cultivate. To add color and a little peppery flavor to salads, pastries, and desserts, sprinkle the petals over. Their petals' yellow-orange hue can also be used to organically color food and textiles like wool and silk. The most intriguing application for calendula flowers, though, is in skincare. The entire flower head possesses antibacterial, antifungal, antiviral, anti-inflammatory, and antiseptic qualities. Calendula can aid in accelerating the healing process when applied to mild burns, rashes, wounds, and abrasions. It is a fantastic ingredient for soothing, natural skincare because of these qualities, especially if you have eczema or inflamed skin.

Use of calendula in skincare

- Aids in acne and pimple eradication
- Encourages the healing of small wounds, cuts, and scrapes.
- Relieves eczema and itchy skin

• Hastens the recovery of mild burns like sunburns.

•It treats cold sores, chapped lips, and dry skin.

• A delicate astringent

• Handmade soap that is naturally colored

• Calendula encourages skin recovery

Calendula flowers contain polysaccharides, flavonoids, triterpenes, resins, carotenes, and other substances according to science. These substances aid in the recovery of injured and inflamed skin, including rashes, eczema, acne, and minor wounds. Calendula substantially doubled the speed of animal wound healing in one study.

Calendula most likely functions by facilitating the rapid formation of granulation tissue in wounds. This moist reddish-pink tissue seals the incision, guards against infection, and kick-starts the healing process. Calendula aids in the healing and soothing of burns in addition to cuts and wounds, and its anti-inflammatory effects lessen discomfort and swelling. Additionally, a promising study demonstrates that calendula can slow the development of malignancies.

Calendula is normally safe to use, so you can treat skin conditions in toddlers and adults with calendula flowers. Calendula is a member of the Asteraceae family, though, and some people may be allergic to it. Please use caution if you are allergic to ragweed, chrysanthemums, or daisies. Calendula may be harmful to you if you're pregnant or nursing.

Purchasing calendula flowers is the quickest way to obtain them. At farmers' markets, I've occasionally seen them provided fresh, but normally they're sold dry. Make sure they've been grown organically and that they're from a reliable source if you're purchasing them online. One approach to determining if they are safe for skincare is to request an MSDS from the retailer (material safety data sheet). If they don't, the calendula they utilize could not be of a high enough caliber to be used in cosmetics and medications. This datasheet won't typically be available from small-scale local producers, but that's okay. The large bulk herbal providers are the ones you should be on the lookout for.

Calendula officinalis is typically used to identify calendula on packaging. There are over 100 cultivars, but the ones with the highest resin content are the best for skincare. Resina and Erfurter Orangefarbige are both great options, but finding this information might be challenging. If you're fortunate, the supplier might be able to tell you the cultivar's name, although this information is typically only provided when purchasing calendula directly from the farmer.

Growing Calendula officinalis

It could be wiser to grow it yourself if you want to be sure you're utilizing a therapeutic type. Calendula is fairly simple to grow, although it does require exposure to the outdoors. That might be in the garden, a flowerbed, a container, or a window box. Their golden petals are not only harvestable from early spring to early winter (and in milder regions, year-round), but they also bring cheer and decorative color. Calendula officinalis is the best flower for skincare if you can only plant one. This cheery and simple-to-grow flower, often known as the pot marigold, has a variety of functions. Since the plants are hardy, they can produce blossoms from May until the first frost. The flowers can be any hue, from buttery yellow to brilliant orange. The best part is that flowers generate more fragrance the more you choose them. It thrives in most open environments and will grow in almost any garden. It is a flower that benefits from being ignored and will develop more effectively if left unattended. You can pluck the blooms once they are in bloom and utilize them to create restorative natural skincare products.

- Appropriate for all zones

- Easy to grow and fuss-free
- Apricot, yellow, and orange blooms
- Complete sun to light shade
- Most soil types, however fertile and well-drained, are preferred.
- Height of the plant: 45-60cm (18-24")
- From late April till the first frost, flowers appear.

Planting seeds of calendula

Despite being a native of the Mediterranean, Calendula officinalis has spread throughout the temperate world due to its hardiness. It thrives in a variety of soil conditions and may even withstand light shade. However, they thrive in sunny locations, especially on well-drained soil. The seahorse-like seeds should be sown in the spring or autumn. You'll see blossoms much earlier if you sow them in the autumn because it will give the plants a head start. The ideal germination temperature for calendula seeds is between 15 and 25 °C (59-77F). If the temperature is lower or higher than this, you might not see many seedlings sprout. In a tray or module filled with one part perlite (or grit) mixed with three parts multipurpose compost in the fall, sow six to eight weeks before the first frost. Add horticultural grit to the topdress, water it in, and keep it moist in a well-lit area. 1.25cm (1/2") of soil should be used to sow the seeds. Leaves will start to appear 6–15 days after sowing. The plants will overwinter well with protection from the cold and slugs, and you can put them outside after the last spring frost. If you're growing them in a tray, you should definitely plant them separately in modules before winter. Calendula seeds can also be sown in modules in the spring. If you're starting them indoors or in a heated greenhouse, use the same steps above and seed 6–8 weeks prior to the final date of frost. Sow after the latest date of the typical frost if your greenhouse is not heated.

Calendula Planting in the Garden

Although it may grow in most types of soil, calendula does best in fertile, well-drained soil. When you plant or sow flowers outdoors, keep this in mind if you want a lot of blooms. Although they can tolerate some shade, I wouldn't recommend planting them there. Despite what some sites may claim, these Mediterranean plants actually prefer the sun. Harden off your baby plants and plant them outside when

They are two inches tall. If you can offer them 1-2 feet in all directions, they'll be able to reach their maximum potential.

Planting Calendula Seeds Directly

Direct sowing in April is quite easy. Plant seeds in rows 18" apart between March and May, well after the last frost. When the young plants reach an inch in height, thin them to a distance of around 15 cm (6 inches) apart to protect them from slugs using beer traps or another natural method.

Allow the plants to continue growing, then thin them to a spacing of 30-60 cm (1-2 feet) until they reach 2-3" in height. The surplus ones can be dug up and planted elsewhere or given away. Weaker plants should be placed in the compost pile.

The above is general advice for planting. Personally, I prefer to plant my calendula in denser plantings that are either spread out over a larger area or grown in a row with plants spaced only a few inches apart. I don't thin them out when they are broadcast or allowed to self-sow. Without outside intervention, they resolve themselves.

Calendula as a plant companion

Calendula can be scattered throughout the garden to encourage the growth of other plants, even if you're like me and grow them for their own benefit. They can draw beneficial plants as well as insects away from valuable vegetables.

Calendula is frequently cultivated in gardens alongside vegetables that require pollination in order to produce fruit or vegetables. Insects are drawn to the colorful blooms, and while they're there, they'll gladly flit over to pollinate the cucumbers, zucchinis, and pumpkins. The edible plants that the companion plant, calendula officinalis, grows well with include:

- Asparagus: it keeps asparagus beetles away.

- Squash and pumpkins draw pollinators to their blossoms.

- Lettuce, kale, cabbages, and other leafy greens deter aphids from landing on these vegetables.

The drawback of calendula is that slugs and snails enjoy hiding in their dense foliage since it is so wet. In other words, you shouldn't plant them right close to something you don't want to be wiped out.

Despite being occasionally referred to as a marigold or "pot marigold," calendula is not closely related to the common marigold you might be more familiar with. It has several recommended partner plants because it is a Tagetes.

Tips for cultivating calendula

You can directly sow into soil that has compost or composted manure as mulch. If not, wait until the plants are about an inch or two tall before adding your preferred mulch. Bring the mulch up to within an inch of the plant, but avoid covering the base of the plant. Mulch will prevent weed growth and keep the soil underneath moist.

Aftercare for calendula is really minimal. My major piece of advice for cultivating them is to let them alone—aside from collecting the flowers—as much as possible. Stunted development and other difficulties are brought on by overwatering and overfeeding. They will happily grow and blossom all summer long if you leave them alone.

You can prune your plants if they start to grow tall and spindly. To pinch back to a leaf node, use your fingers or a pair of scissors. Keep your plants at a height of no more than 60 cm (two feet). They use less water, stay bushier and healthier longer, and stand up better to wind.

Later in the growing season, calendula can experience aphid problems in terms of pests. If you see an infestation, use soapy water to spray the aphids off. When water-stressed or grown in close proximity to one another, calendula can also develop a fungus called powdery mildew.

Calendula in Containers Growing

Calendula is flexible and will thrive in window boxes, outdoor pots, and other containers. Along with the flower harvest, they'll add a dash of color for the most of the year. Make sure the compost has sufficient drainage and is moist while growing in pots. Add one part perlite or grit, one part vermiculite, and three parts multipurpose to get a nice mixture. Vermiculite aerates while also retaining water, Perlite adds drainage, compost provides nutrients and a surface for root growth. After planting, compact the compost and sprinkle horticultural grit on top. This will prevent weeds from colonizing the surface and help the compost retain water.

Calendula Blooming Period

After germination, calendula plants will start to bloom 45–60 days later, and as long as the blooms are regularly picked, they will continue to bloom. In fact, if you're rigorous about dead-heading, they'll bloom all throughout the summer and fall. Some plants will even bloom into the winter in milder areas.

On the other hand, you might notice that your plants stop blooming in warm climates or during a scorching summer. They are fortifying themselves against the heat and will resume flowering when the weather cools in the fall. The blossoms of the calendula plant aren't simply for decoration; they also have health benefits for the skin and are delicious. That means plucking flowers while they are at their best not only encourages new flowers to blossom, but also allows you to use the blooms. Calendula is one of my favorite ingredients to use in handcrafted soap and skincare products. The petals can also be used to flavor and color food preparations.

Various Single and Double Flower Types

The flowers themselves are typically 2-3" in diameter and range in color from yellow to vivid orange. Calendula officinalis comes in a variety of forms, some of which bloom as single blooms and others with double rows of petals. Some cultivars, like Fiesta Gitano, produce flowers with semi-double to fully double petals that are both yellow and orange in color. Calendula seeds can also be purchased in mixtures, allowing you to grow single, double, yellow, and orange blooms in a single row. The majority of the 100 or so varieties of calendula officinalis have been developed for the decorative market. However, all cultivars of flowers have edible and therapeutic petals. It simply means that the more resinous types are better suitable for health and skincare.

• Double with orange flowers, Erfurter Orangefarbige. The ideal cultivar to use for herbal and skin care products is this one.

• Resina, a solitary flower with yellow pistils and petals. Another excellent cultivar for using herbs.

• Orange Single – a single with orange petals and a pistil

• Double and orange-red with a dark pistil, Indian Prince

• Double and yellowy-pink Pink Surprise

Calendula: An Annual or a Perennial?

Although calendula is essentially a short-lived perennial, it can survive for at least a few years if it is not damaged by a strong frost. In zone 8, a couple of my plants survive each winter, albeit occasionally their lowest stems turn dark and lanky. Calendula is an annual that can only be grown in zones 7 and lower. This indicates that it will most likely die off and require resowing every year. Fortunately, they generate a lot of seeds and, given the chance, will self-seed. The next year, a new crop of calendula will grow there thanks to these self-sown seeds, which overwinter. You can even save seeds and begin planting again the following spring.

Gathering of calendula seeds

It is simple to gather and store calendula seeds directly from the plant. After making the initial seed purchase, you shouldn't need to buy seeds again. A few of the blooms should be allowed to bloom, lose their petals, and change into seed heads. The seed heads can be trimmed off the plant before the seeds are discharged as they grow and turn brown. Cut the seed heads off by themselves or with a stem that is at least six inches long. Cutting only a small portion of the stem may be simpler, but it will also take away from the plant's potential for future flowering. Place the flower heads in a brown paper bag after tying the clipped stems with a string. To prevent it from falling off, tie it. Dry the stems by hanging upside down in a warm, airy location. After this, shake the bag vigorously to remove most of the seeds. Tease the others away if necessary. Simply take off the seed heads and store them in a brown paper bag. Store the bag in a warm, dry area. Pull the seeds off the heads with your fingers once they are completely dry. In bags or jars, keep dried calendula seeds away from direct sunlight in a cool, dry location. Use within six years for the optimum germination.

Calendula in a nutshell

- Hardy annual in cooler zones, perennial in mild climates
- Orange to yellow blooms
- About 100 varieties

• Used as a vulnerary by herbalists (wound healer)

• Beneficial for treating acne and eczema

Additionally known as marigolds or pot marigolds

Preservation in oil

Calendula can be prepared and preserved in oil, which is one of the best methods. The petals of the dried flowers release their curative constituents into the liquid when you seep them in light oils like grape seed or sweet almond.

Fill a glass jar with dried calendula flower heads and/or petals to produce calendula oil. Then, add enough of your preferred liquid carrier oil to completely cover the flowers in the jar. Remember to shake the jar every couple of days and seal it before storing it in a warm location for 2-4 weeks. If you want to infuse the oil in a window, it is crucial to protect the oil from UV radiation by placing the jar within a brown paper bag. The oil may be harmed by UV rays and become rancid as a result.

After the allotted time has passed, strain the oil from the dried flowers. Because the oil will have been absorbed by the dried flowers, be careful to squeeze out every last drop. Place in a cold, dark area after bottling into dark glass jars. The shelf life of calendula oil is one year or until the carrier oil's best-by date. It can be used as a skin serum, to make homemade soap, skin lotion, or salves.

'Aloe Vera' (Aloe barbadensis).

Aloe Vera grows effectively indoors if your climate isn't warm enough to allow for outside growth. It leaves contain a gel that can be used to treat burns and lessen swelling. Aloe can also be used as an oil-free moisturizer, although frequent use can cause your skin to become very dry. It is preferable to incorporate aloe Vera into a mild lotion for everyday skin treatment. Open the leaves and scoop out the gel to extract. Aloe can be used alone or in creams and lotions, but it must first be blended and/or strained.

Formula for Organic Aloe Face Cream with Directions

I use this face lotion every day because it is packed with ingredients that are good for the skin. It is manufactured with just natural ingredients and is ideal for people with normal to oily skin. It is also simple and affordable to create, and it is incredibly sensitive. Aloe Vera, which you can scrape from your own plant's leaf, is one of the constituents. You can use store-bought gel if you don't have one. Aloe, a mild astringent, aids in soothing inflammation and lowering redness. You are presumably aware of its application to sunburns. Rose-hip, which is high in antioxidants and utilized in anti-aging formulae, sweet almond, light oil that is frequently used in massage, and Shea butter, rich and creamy solid oil, are the oils used in this recipe.

Recommended Equipment

- A piece of clear glass, like a mason jar
- A double boiler can be made out of two pans
- Kitchen spout
- Small dishes and spoons
- Milk blender

•1 120ml (4.1 oz) airless pump bottle; these can be sanitized, cleaned, and used repeatedly.

•Digital pocket scale

• (optional) - If you're measuring in grams rather than teaspoons, I've provided both dimensions.

Recipe for Organic Aloe Face Cream

Approximately 120 ml (4.1oz)

The following elements are stated in three stages. These three main categories of ingredients will be added at various stages of the procedure. The "Oil Phase" is made up of the primary oils, the "Water Phase" is made up of the water and the items that need to dissolve, and the "Cooling Phase" is made up of the heat-sensitive substances.

Oil Phase

- Olivem 1000*, 3 g (1.5 tsp), is the emulsifier.
- Organic Sweet Almond oil, which weighs 10 g (2.5 tsp) and is easily absorbed.
- 0.5 g (1/8 tsp) of organic shea butter, a creamy, rich solid oil
- 2 grams (or half a teaspoon) of organic rosehip seed oil

Water Phase

- 1/4 cup of distilled water, 70 ml.

Cooling Period

• Fresh or bottled 7 g (2 tsp) organic aloe vera from the leaf

• Organic Honey, 4 g (1/2 tsp), draws moisture to your skin

• 1 g of organic rose geranium essential oil (20 drops) (optional)

• 0.5 g (1/8 tsp) of Vitamin E Oil each capsule (optional)

• 1.5 g (1/2 tsp.) A preservative permitted for use in organic skincare is Geogard Ultra. Additional name: Microguard

* Olivem 1000 is a certified organic beauty product, however it can change. I've used it successfully on its own for this recipe, but I can't guarantee that your lotion won't split if you change the components or the amounts.

Step 1: Get the aloe ready

To treat sunburns, many individuals keep an aloe vera plant. Fresh aloe can also be used as a mild astringent in skincare products to help treat eczema, acne, and other skin conditions. It is also naturally oil-free, making it the perfect moisturizer for nourishing oily skin.

Cut a section of the aloe leaf that is three inches long and a half inch wide. Close the plant's wound with a gentle squeeze to promote healing.

With a potato peeler or small knife, remove the leaf's outer layer, then crush the stiff gel into a liquidier consistency. Large lumps should be avoided as they will find their way into the lotion. If you cut off more than you need, measure out what you need and keep the unpeeled leaves in the fridge for up to a week. For three days, the aloe gel can be stored in the refrigerator.

Step 2: the oil phase

The oil phase materials should be placed in a small pan and melted together in a double boiler. While stirring, float the pan in a second pan of simmering water.

Step 3: Water phase

After bringing the water to a boil, measure out the precise quantity into a heat-resistant, transparent container. Please be aware that even if you start with the precise amount specified in the recipe, some will evaporate. Therefore, it is preferable to boil more than is required before measuring.

The Geogard Ultra should be placed in a dish with a small amount of hot water. Place it back with the remaining "Cooling Phase" ingredients after stirring with a spoon until all the ingredients have dissolved.

Step 4: Combination of the water and oil phases.

Consider the water and oil phase temperatures. The oil should be within ten degrees of that temperature and the water should be around 160F (70C). Set the jar in the pan of hot water to reheat it up if your water starts to cool down too much.

When the conditions are ideal, immerse your milk frother in the water phase, and while swirling with the frother, slowly pour the melted oil into the water. Don't forget to add every last drop.

The mixture should now be pulverized with the frother until it is opaque but still slightly runny, as seen in the example below. Be careful not to bring the frother near the lotion's surface while it is pulsing. This could result in unwelcome air bubbles in your lotion.

A word on temperature when preparing lotions: I've heard a number of different temps, "Heating and Holding," and other methods recommended. The temperatures required for lotion production are just warm enough to completely melt the oils for the oil phase, and the water phase needs to be hotter than the oils' melting point. This prevents the oils from freezing when they contact the water. As it turns out, temperature has minimal impact on the preservative's ability to permanently kill bacteria in lotions.

Step 5: Cooling

Rest the lotion until it reaches a temperature of around 113F (45C) or the jar feels lukewarm to the touch. Throughout the process of chilling, stir the lotion occasionally. When the temperature is appropriate, thoroughly whisk the lotion before adding the components for the "Cooling phase." Once the final lotion has reached room temperature, pour it into your airless dispenser and cover it. This prevents condensation from forming.

You can now use your organic aloe face cream. It can have a shelf life of roughly 18 months when used with the preservative and airless dispenser. Remove the top of your airless dispenser when it is empty, and then push the section that rises as you use the lotion down with a bamboo skewer. To sterilize it, thoroughly wash it and then put it in the dishwasher. Like new and prepared to receive additional lotion.

Echinacea (Echinacea purpurea).

Extract from echinacea helps heal acne, lessen inflammation, and hasten skin regeneration. Additionally, it has a lovely blossom that would look lovely in any yard. Use the roots' decoction or the blooms' water infusion as a toner or beverage. The liquid can also be used to create creams and lotions. It works best as a tincture for curing acne.

Comfrey (Symphytum offinale).

Comfrey is a fantastic choice for treating inflamed skin because its leaves and blossoms have potent anti-inflammatory qualities. These components can be used to create infusions that can be used as a toner or in creams and lotions. It works particularly well to promote skin healing and cure skin eruptions such eczema, psoriasis, acne, and others. These days, we more often use the leaves of this plant as a herbal oil than the roots. Please be aware that comfrey should not be ingested.

Causes of Acne

Acne and black/whiteheads are brought on by a number of conditions that stimulate oil production. Stress or hormonal changes (such as those brought on by adolescence or menopause) may be to blame, but the ultimate result is sebum-clogged pores. The often unproblematic Propionibacterium acnes bacteria subsequently starts to cause problems. As they accumulate inside the blocked pore, your body sends cells there to deal with the infestation. A raised red bump that may or may not resemble a head is the end outcome.

Reduce your stress levels, stay hydrated, and treat your skin gently if you have pimples. Don't give up trying to locate the correct treatment for you because your skin may respond better to some than others.

Herbs for Oily Skin and Acne

Green tea (Camellia sinensis).

Contains anti-oxidants that can reduce inflammation, stop bacterial development, and regulate sebum (oil) production. Use fresh or dried tea leaves infusions in creams, lotions, or as a toner for the face.

Lavender (Lavandula angustifolia).

Lavender is a widespread and aromatic garden shrub with antibacterial and anti-inflammatory qualities. This makes it advantageous for people who have inflammatory and irritated skin. Cuts, burns, and abrasions have all been demonstrated to heal more quickly when treated with lavender oil. Make an oil infusion from dried flowers to use in creams, lotions, or as a facial toner. To produce lavender water, you can also combine water and alcohol (or witch hazel) with fresh or dried flowers. Here's how to grow lavender for recipes involving skin care.

English Lavender Growing Instructions

English lavender can be grown for a variety of reasons, and if the correct conditions are provided, it can also be done pretty simply. It can be cultivated as feature plants spread throughout the garden, in pots on its own, or in hedges. You may utilize their blossoms in everything from food dishes to crafts and homemade treatments. They can also be used to define margins and borders in a garden. The ability of lavender to attract pollinators is another reason to cultivate it; when the summer blooms open, bees are actually humming all around them. I cultivate a variety of English lavender varieties, including hybrids, and through the years, I've discovered a few things about them. Learn how to cultivate English lavender in your yard with the advice I've provided here. You'll have years of sweet-scented foliage and flowers that you and your neighborhood wildlife will enjoy if you plant them in the proper place.

An Overview of English Lavender

- Perennial evergreen

- Leaves that range from green to gray, with generally purple blooms

- Flowers have a strong fragrance.

- There are 47 varieties of lavender.

- Plants can live up to 15 years.

- There are around 40 different cultivars of the plant.

The best lavender for skincare and cooking is English lavender.

There are 47 different varieties of lavender. One such plant is English lavender. Over 40 different cultivars of the species exist, and their flowers come in a variety of hues, from light purple to deep blue-purple to pale pink.

There are other names for English lavender, including common lavender and Lavandula angustifolia, which is the botanical name. Contrary to its more common moniker, it actually originates from the Mediterranean and the Middle East and is not native to the British Isles. Locations with damp winters and lengthy, scorching summers the following are some of the most well-liked cultivars in Britain:

- Hidcote', a little cultivar that is small and has deep purple blossoms.

- The pale pink blooms and grey-green foliage of "Little Lottie"

- "Vera," a vintage cultivar with deep lavender-blue flowers

- Gertrude Jekyll's favorite flower was "Munstead," a loose, light purple bloom.

• Lavandula x intermedia 'Grosso,' a large, gorgeous hybrid lavender with lots of flowers

However, English lavender is frequently labeled without a cultivar designation and just as that. If you want to know the cultivar name, it can be a little annoying, but I have a few 'nameless' plants in my garden. They've made me joyful, and I've even multiplied them to grow additional plants.

A Guide to Growing English Lavender

If you provide the proper climate, soil, and sun exposure, lavender is simple to grow. Since I have lavender that thrives in somewhat acidic clay soil, you can even push the limits with some of these!

•It grows in zones 5-8 as a perennial.

• Appreciates full sun

• It's Neutral to alkaline soil that drains well

• Does not enjoy humidity or damp feet

• The plant's height is 1-3 feet, and its spread is 1–5 feet.

The ideal type of soil for English lavender

As long as you give English lavender the proper soil and environment, it can be grown very easily. It prefers planting in a sunny location with alkaline pH free-draining soil (6.7-7.3). As a result, you can frequently observe it flourishing in arid, chalky soil. When I was a resident of London, I frequently strolled past a front garden where the most incredible lavender was growing. It developed on the opposite side of a small, dilapidated stone wall, which likely provided it with shade and the ideal soil conditions.

Garden lime can be added to the soil to raise pH if it is more acidic. Additionally, English lavender enjoys a dry environment, so make sure it has good drainage. If your soil is heavy, think about growing lavender along a ridge that has good drainage. By incorporating compost, grit, gravel, and stones into the soil and drawing it up, you can make this.

Climate Conditions for English Lavender

In temperate to desert areas, English lavender thrives and enjoys dry to damp soil. In fact, if it receives too much water, it may not flourish. English lavender dislikes humid environments and struggles to grow there even if it prefers warmer climates.

English lavender can endure frigid winter temperatures as low as -10°F (-23°C), although other types of lavender may be less resilient. As a result, it qualifies as a hardy perennial evergreen that may grow in zones 5 to 9. Although most English lavender cultivars don't thrive in zones 10 and up, I've read some internet accounts of folks who have. In order to be certain, I believe we need to grow just one plant. In the event that English lavender doesn't thrive in your climate, don't invest in more than that.

Advice for Growing English Lavender

Lavender plants are widely available at garden centers, but you may also grow them from seed the year before you intend to plant them. Lavender may be grown from seed, but it will take them a year or more to mature before they are ready to be planted in the garden.

Let's imagine you've discovered the ideal location in your garden for English lavender: it receives plenty of light, the soil has the ideal pH and is free-draining, and it's mid to late April. Planting time has come.

Standard-sized lavender cultivars should be placed three feet apart for an airier planting and a foot apart to form a hedge. Given that dwarf varieties are smaller plants by nature, you can plant them a little closer together. They should be placed in a hole at the same height as in their pot, and the hole should be well-watered. After they become established, the soil should stop needing moisture, so stop watering them.

Pruning English Lavender

Many people are hesitant to prune their English lavender plants, but it's a skill that anybody can learn. Keep in mind that lavender rarely produces new leaves on old wood. You can somewhat reduce the amount of greenery there, but don't remove too much. Create the plant's shape to fit it, whether you want a spherical plant, a lavender hedge, or something else

To keep the plants' vigor and shape, start trimming them in their second year. Trim the spent flower stalks after flowering to shape the plants. Additionally, I put off doing this task until later and instead prune my plants in the very early spring, when after the first flush of new leaves appears. When you reach the first of these brand-new, fresh leaves, continue running your fingertips along the stem. Just above it, and cut. Remove any stems or branches that are brown and dead as well.

English Lavender Container Growing Techniques

Lavender thrives in pots because it enjoys drier surroundings. The ideal terracotta pots have diameters between 12 and 18 inches. Grow English lavender in a free-draining mixture that contains two parts multipurpose compost and one part vermiculite or grit. If you want to make the surface look nice and prevent weed seeds from growing, top dress with grit.

After the first couple of years, feeding with an organic slow-release feed during the summer is optional. Although it generally won't require it, if it appears dejected, it might require a little something extra. First, make sure you are not overwatering it.

Keep English lavender moist when growing in pots during the summer, but let it dry out in the winter. Keep in mind that colder temperatures can cause the soil within to remain wet, and it dislikes wet feet. Place your potted lavender inside a greenhouse if you have one for the winter; the slightly warmer temperature will make them happier.

English lavender doesn't grow well indoors, which is another thing to keep in mind. Your potted plants will thrive better in the garden, on your balcony, or in a window box. Growing lavender in a container can be the perfect answer if you want to use it in skincare products.

Bodhi Root (Arctium lappa).

Burdock is a special herb for skincare because it should primarily be used internally. It is a purifying plant that treats acne, boils, psoriasis, and eczema from the inside out. For up to a month, consume a daily infusion of the root.

Thyme (Thymus vulgaris).

Thyme is more successful at treating acne than the most popular acne treatment ingredient, benzoyl peroxide, according to recent studies. In order to conduct the study, scientists utilized a tincture, which they apparently applied to spots.

Within five minutes, the bacterium that causes blemishes was eliminated.

Lemon juice.

Citrus' astringent characteristics might help you get rid of extra oil and brighten your skin when applied with cotton wool.

Aloe vera

Aloe vera is not only a soothing toner and oil-free moisturizer, but its fresh gel also aids in healing and inflammation. Try to use it sparingly as a spot treatment rather than as a daily moisturizer since overuse can result in dryness. It is ideal to use every day if it is formulated into a balanced lotion like this one.

Skincare for mature skin

The firmness and radiance of mature skin are absent, and it might be sensitive and dry. Additionally, it could have hyper-pigmentation, bigger pores, and wrinkles. Treatments should be moderate, and you should take steps to prevent dehydration and more sun damage.

Roses (Rosa).

Rosewater is an excellent toner for all skin types because it has a mild astringent. Given that it is mild and moisturizing, it is especially beneficial for aged skin. It also has a fantastic scent. The by-product of distilling rose petals to generate essential oil is true rose water. However, you can use this infusion technique to create your own hack version. Rose petals from either cultivated or wild roses can be used.

Using fresh rose petals learn how to make rose water toner.

Since ancient times, people have utilized rose water as a mild yet effective astringent. The common person would have used this technique to make calming and cleansing skin toners long before we had commercially available rose water.

It's really that easy! It helps to cleanse, tighten, and reduce redness and inflammation when applied to the skin with cotton pad or spray bottle. It is a wonderful addition to creams and lotions because it is also quite delicate and suitable for use on most skin types.

This recipe is an infusion since true rosewater must be prepared by distillation. However, a rose petal infusion can offer the same skin-loving treatment as some of the more expensive remedies. Rose hydrosol and absolute are lovely extracts that are good for the skin, but they can be expensive. You can make a natural skin toner with a lovely aroma with this recipe for nearly nothing. Rose petals and pure water are all that are required.

Home-made rose water toner

Rose water should have a subtle rose scent after the process is complete. Start with antique or wild roses if you want even a small amount of the aroma to linger. Your rose water will smell more fragrant the more fragrant the roses are. However, any organic rose petals would do. Rose petals from flowers should not be used in bouquets, nevertheless. In most cases, toxic pesticides and fungicides are applied on flowers that are sold as ornaments.

The color of the rose toner will be influenced by the color of the rose petals, which is another item to take into account. It will be pink if you use pink or red roses, clear if you use white roses, and yellow if you use orange rose petals. Although I personally wouldn't claim that one is better than the other based only on color, I do favor using pink or red roses.

For a lovely fragrance, use wild rose petals.

Any of the wild roses are my preferred rose to use for this dish. There are around six different varieties, but the rosa rugosa (beach rose) and rosa canina on my porch are the only two (dog rose). Pick the petals straight from the bloom while foraging for wild roses, leaving the hip intact. You may come in the fall to gather them for rose-hip tea or syrup if it has already been pollinated. Place your palm over the flower of a garden rose and gently peel off all the petals. Generally speaking, if the flower has been in bloom for a few days, they tend to fall off quite readily.

Making Rose Water:

Pick around three cups of rose petals to produce rosewater. To let any insects escape, set them outside on a tea towel. Give them about 30 minutes.

The rose petals should then be added to a saucepan. If you'd like, you can stuff it with rose petals all the way to the top. Just enough water (ideally distilled) should be added to the pan to cover the flower petals. As soon as the majority of the color has disappeared from the petals, cover the pan and heat it on low. Keep the water from simmering at all costs; it will only take a few minutes. The healthy qualities and color of a flower can be destroyed by excessive heat.

Rose Water for the Skin and using it

Discard the remaining rose petals after the petals have significantly faded and strain the liquid through a fine-mesh strainer. Once the rose water toner has cooled, pour it into a clean jar and store it there in the refrigerator until you're ready to use it. It will last for about a week if stored in this manner.

Use a cotton pad to apply rose water toner on its own, or use a little spray bottle to mist your face. It has a beautiful scent, offers immediate refreshment, and lessens redness and inflammation. You'll see that it also picks up a lot of dirt and makeup when you apply it on a pad. If the rose water is aromatic enough, you can smell roses coming off your skin afterward, and your skin feels incredibly clean.

Rose Water as a Moisturizer Ingredient

Use the rose water toner within six months if you want it to survive much longer; otherwise, freeze it into ice cubes. You may maintain that rosy sweetness in this way without the use of preservatives. You would need to apply a preservative if you wanted to keep this handmade rose water preserved on the shelf. You might need to adjust the recipe to lower the pH because many products on the market only function if the product is within a specific pH range.

Reminder: Roses from grocery store or florist bouquets should never be used for skincare or food flowers. Sadly, they are treated with pesticides and other chemicals while they are growing. You can use organically grown roses that you have cultivated yourself or food-grade rose petals that are fresh or dried for this recipe.

Herbs Astringent for Skincare

Toners and astringents are liquid products that remove excess oil, tighten skin, and minimize pore size. They work particularly well for oily skin, but they can also help firm skin.

Witch hazzel (Hamamelis).

Witch hazel, a common ingredient in cosmetic toners, has a lot of astringent tannins by nature. These aids in, skin tightening and oil removal. By first creating a decoction of the bark and combining it with alcohol, such as 80 proof vodka, you can create a tincture. The smaller twigs from recent growth work best, but dry bark can still be used. As a natural toner, use a leaf infusion with water.

Yarrow (Achillea millefolium).

There are "weeds" in every garden, but some are more beneficial than others. You might choose to promote yarrow, a typical wild plant utilized in herbal medicine, in a skincare garden. The leaves and petals can be infused in water to make an astringent toner that helps eliminate oil, evens out skin tone, and soothes inflammation.

Citrus balm (Melissa officinalis).

This is a plant with a lemony, minty flavor that can be used as a cooling toner for greasy, acne-prone skin. Use an infusion of the leaves in water as a toner, and use an infusion in water or oil to make mild lotions. Lemon balm extract works well in lip balms and cold sore creams since it has antiviral qualities as well.

Rosemary (Rosmarinus officinalis).

All skin types can benefit from an aromatic astringent made from an infusion of rosemary leaves. By increasing blood flow to the skin, it also aids in the promotion of healing. You can make massage oils, toners, creams, hair rinses, balms, and lotions using an oil or water infusion of this herb.

Treating Dry Skin

Skin conditions, environmental factors, dehydration, medications, and the usage of particular cosmetics can all contribute to dry skin. Aloe Vera is an example of a plant that can over dry skin even when used excessively in skincare. Drinking enough water will help your skin retain moisture, which is the first step in properly moisturizing it. Keep your face away from too hot water and moisturize with soft creams and lotions. Extracts from these plants have beneficial properties.

Herbs that are hydrating for the skin

Violet (Viola odorata or Viola canina).

Violet leaf and blossom extract is juicy and nourishing, with a little astringent scent. Violets are excellent for dry skin and also have anti-inflammatory and wound-healing properties. To prepare creams, lotions, balms, massage oils, and toners, infuse fresh plant material in water or oil.

Common Plantain (Plantago major or Plantago lanceolata).

Plantain leaves provide moisturizing mucilage, making them another "weed" that thrives in most gardens. You can use it as a powerful skin healer to speed the recovery of cuts and bruises. For usage in salves, creams, lotions, balms, and massage oils, prepare the leaves by infusing them with water or oil.

Roses (Rosa).

Rosewater or a rose petal infusion moisturizes and revitalizes the skin. Rose extract is great for all skin types, but it works especially well for delicate dry and aging skin.

Marsh Mallow (Althaea officinalis).

Rich quantities of mucilage, pectin, and sugars found in marshmallow roots, leaves, and flowers soothe and moisturize the skin. However, the concentration is higher in the roots. Make smooth lotions and creams by soaking the roots in cold water overnight.

Skin Inflammation Treatment

Numerous factors, including allergies, the menstrual cycle, poor health, or the aftereffects of a night out dancing, can cause skin to feel irritated. Use these herbs to make easy herbal rinses or one of the recommended skin treatments for skincare. Each will aid in reducing inflammation, puffiness, and redness.

Plants for Inflamed, Red, and Puffy Skin

Speedwell (Veronica chamaedrys).

A flower used as an anti-inflammatory to reduce eczema and other skin diseases' redness and itching. In some places, it grows wild, yet it adds beauty to any garden. Use the leaves and blossoms' water infusion as a toner or in creams and lotions.

French chamomile (Matricaria recutita).

It is a soft herb that is used to calm dry, itchy skin brought on by dermatitis and eczema. However, it can be applied to all skin types. Make balms, creams, lotions, toners, or massage oils with oil or water infusions. Avoid taking chamomile if you have a ragweed (ragwort) allergy.

Cucumber (Cucumis sativus)

Cucumbers are a typical garden vegetable whose moist flesh tightens skin, calms inflammation, and decreases puffiness. To soothe, tighten, and brighten dark circles under the eyes, place slices of cucumber over the area. Cucumber can also be infused with water and used in creams and lotions, or pureed as a face mask.

Chickweed (Stellaria media)

Chickweed is a very prevalent weed in many gardens and works well as an anti-inflammatory. To produce balms, salves, creams, lotions, and other beauty items, infuse the leaves in water or oil. It can also be used to lessen inflammation, ease itchiness, and lessen redness.

Gradual Change in Color

Some skin care herbs might aid in gradually lightening or darkening hair, moles, and nails. You can use them with the confidence that they are natural and fully safe, even though their effects aren't as immediate as chemical alternatives.

Natural Darkening Plants for Lightening Skin and hair

Elderflower (Sambucus).

Elderflowers bloom from late May to early June, and you may use them to flavor sweets and sweet drinks. It is less well recognized that flower infusions in water or oil can be used to lighten scars, age spots, and scarring. Additionally anti-inflammatory, the extract can help moisturize older skin.

Sage (Salvia officinalis).

In addition to using it to cleanse greasy skin, you can use this herb as a rinse for dark hair. Apply the water-infused fresh or dried leaves to your hair every day. It can progressively darken hair, albeit it won't color it permanently. However, gray or coarse hair may be color-resistant. For heightened darkening effects, you might also combine it with rosemary, ground black walnut hulls, nettles, and coffee.

Rosemary (Rosmarinus officinalis).

Sage and rosemary both work well to help darken hair. Use an infusion of water as a hair rinse.

French chamomile (Matricaria recutita).

A natural hair lightener is chamomile. As a hair rinse or in leave-in conditioners, use an infusion of the blossoms in water. If you wish to maximize the lighting power of chamomile, use it simultaneously with lemon juice.

Green tea (Camellia sinensis).

Green tea's high antioxidant content has been demonstrated to assist in repairing skin harmed by aging and external stressors. Use the water infusion as a toner, to drink as tea, or to make creams and lotions.

Lady's shawl (Alchemilla vulgaris).

Found in anti-wrinkle creams, lady's mantle helps firm the skin and decrease the size of pores. Use the leaves' water infusion as a toner or as an ingredient in creams and lotions. It is also a herb for women, and you may make a tea out of it to ease menstrual cramps and menopausal symptoms.

Helichrysum (Helichrysum italicum).

Helichrysum's natural anti-inflammatory qualities help to lessen redness and encourage regeneration. Additionally, it works wonders as a skincare ingredient for issues like acne and aging or damaged skin. To reduce fine lines and wrinkles, use the flowers in a tincture, oil, or water infusion. The solutions can be added to creams and lotions or used as toners on their own. Because of its strong aroma, helichrysum is often referred to as the curry plant.

There are several reasons to produce your own herbal skincare products. Some of these include saving money on beauty goods, using herbs from your garden that are already blooming, beginning a business, or simply as a fun weekend hobby. Whatever the motivation, becoming proficient in the use of herbs is a useful and artistic skill to have. Additionally, your skin will appreciate it.

You may safely extract the skin-beneficial qualities of many plants at home. Flavonoids, tannins, mucilage, antioxidants, resins, acids, proteins, and volatile oils are examples of compounds that have these qualities. They might start in flower petals, leaves, bark, roots, or stems, depending on the plant.

You can use the various extracts from each plant to create your own beauty products. The foundation of this piece is the creation of those extracts. Isolating those natural ingredients using straightforward, common techniques is the key to creating DIY herbal skincare products.

This is typically an additional step that you perform before preparing the recipe. Make calendula-infused oil, for instance, and use it to create body balms, lip balms, creams, salt scrubs, bath bombs, and other products. The remainder of this article walks you through herbal skincare recipes and herbal extraction techniques.

Herbal Skincare with Oil

Picking and drying the plant material is typically the first step in making herbal extracts. To create the ingredients for use in beauty recipes, it is further infused into oil, water, or alcohol. However, there are a few situations where you can start with new content.

The Value of Preserving Plant Resources

Flowers, herbs, and fresh produce can all spoil. They are prone to developing mold, rotting, and attracting microorganisms. Despite how tiny it may appear, the water content of the plant material is the major factor. If a broad-spectrum preservative isn't utilized, it promotes bacterial development and can cause your cosmetics to expire.

For instance, fresh aloe Vera gel only keeps well in the refrigerator for 7–10 days. And everyone is aware of how easily a bunch of herbs may become sour and brown. You risk having mold and bacteria forming in your skin cream within days if you use either ingredient without adding a preservative, whether you notice it or not. Learning how to preserve plants and create products that won't deteriorate is the first step in creating secure DIY herbal skincare.

Herbs and Flower Drying

Herbs used in skincare can be used on-the-go longer if they are first dried. Plant material typically has a shelf life of one to two years after drying. The plants can be used at that time to manufacture skincare products by infusing them into oils, water, glycerin, or alcohol.

On a good day, gather herbs late in the morning. When the dew has had time to dry, the volatile oils in the plant are at their highest level. When they are fully open in the afternoon, you pick flowers like chamomile and calendula that open during the day and close at night.

They can be dried in an oven on low heat, on a drying screen, by hanging them on a rack, or in a food dehydrator. To allow the water vapor to escape if you're utilizing the oven approach, prop the oven door open a bit.

Make sure you are aware of the finest methods for drying the plant part you require. Regardless of the method, the plant material must be crisp, completely dry, and room temperature before being placed in jars or zip-top bags for storage.

Oil versus water-soluble

The extraction technique you use will mostly depend on the herb you're using and the final product you're making. Calendula, plantain, and many more herbs happily infuse into a carrier oil. There are compounds that are water-soluble in other herbs and flowers, such as rose petals. Some are soluble in both water and oil.

Flavonoids, polyphenols, organic acids, sugars, and glycosides are all polar chemicals that are drawn to water since it is a polarizing substance. Oil, a non-polar material, extracts fatty acids, lipids, carotenoids, tocopherols, and carotenoids best.

Alcohol is used to prepare tinctures and ethanol alcohol may extract both water- and oil-soluble compounds.

Infused with herbs

Making oil with infused herbs is one of the simplest ways to obtain skin-beneficial compounds from plants. It entails steeping dried herbs and flowers in a carrier oil like coconut oil, sweet almond oil, or olive oil. The oil can be ready in one day or four weeks, depending on which of these you utilize to manufacture it. After that, you can use the oil directly on your skin or to create other products by straining it out. You can incorporate a variety of plants into oil, including:

- The calendula (flower)
- The chamomile (flower)
- Chamomile (leaf)
- Lavandin (flowers)

- Citrus balm (leaf)
- Bananas (leaf)
- Rosary (leaf)
- The Yarrow (leaf)

Massage oil is the simplest application for infused oil. Additionally, you can incorporate it into your regular beauty routine as a serum or as a component in body balms, lip balms, salves, and creams.

Herb-infused Water for Skincare

Although tisane is the correct term for herb-infused water, you might prefer to think of it as herbal tea. Herbal water can be prepared as an infusion or a decoction, and after cooled, it can be used to manufacture skin creams, lotions, and rinses. You may also use a herbal tisane as a serum or toner by spritzing it on your face after cleansing.

Water infusions are prepared in the same manner as a typical cup of herbal tea. The only difference is that you would use more herbal ingredients and occasionally let the tea simmer for a longer period of time. Decoctions are used with harder plant components like bark and roots. Boiling the plant material in water yields a decoction.

The use of rosemary tisane as a hair rinse is thought to promote blood flow, stop dandruff, and lessen hair loss. You can progressively lighten hair using chamomile hair rinses. Tisanes make excellent bases for skin creams and mild toners. Create your own skin care tones using:

•The calendula (flower)

•The chamomile (flower)

•Echinacea (all parts)

• Lavandin (flower)

•Citrus balm (leaf)

- Peppermint (leaf) (leaf)
- Rose (flower and hip)

Skincare Tinctures

The greatest technique to extract the entire range of plant compounds is through tinctures. They normally contain alcohol as the liquid, and when you create them at home, vodka with an 80 proof is most frequently utilized. However, it's not exactly gentle on the skin and can be very drying. Witch hazel that has been purchased can be used to create skin tinctures instead. Witch hazel extract, Hamamelis virginiana, and a trace amount of ethanol alcohol make up this typical skin toner.

Vegetable glycerin can be used to create an even milder tincture. It is a sticky, sweet ingredient used to create healthcare products, particularly creams and lotions. It is really hydrating and won't dry out your skin.

When creating tinctures, the solvent you use should be appropriate for the intended use. Essential oils, alkaloids, glycosides, acids, and bitters can all be extracted best with alcohol. Vinegar and glycerin work better at drawing out more compounds from your herbs.

One of the best ingredients for skincare is a tincture, since it can extract both water-and oil-soluble components from plants. Use tinctures alone or diluted with distilled water as skin toners, to treat minor wounds and pimples, and to add to creams and toners for skin care. Internal skincare tinctures, such as red clover and burdock root, would typically advise you to take such tinctures internally.

However, one thing you can take for breakouts is thyme tincture. It has been demonstrated that thyme kills acne-causing germs more effectively than over-the-counter drugs. Additionally, the alcohol in a tincture aids in pore tightening and disinfection. Additionally, the following ingredients can be used to create tinctures for topical application:

•The calendula (flower)

•Echinacea (root)

• Thyme (leaf)

•Witch hazle (bark)

Making soap with flowers and herbs

I adore decorating soap with fresh and dried herbs as a soap maker. They are quite helpful for organically coloring my bars as well. Every fleck of dried peppermint eventually surrounds itself with a golden halo. Gromwell and alkanet roots give soap a natural purple hue. Poppy seeds make lovely decorations but can also increase the exfoliating properties of soap.

There is some disagreement about whether or not plant therapeutic properties endure the cold or hot process soap-making process. If you want to make soap with infused oil, it's better to either use re-batched soap or melt-and-pour soap like in this recipe.

Cold-process or hot-process soap that has gone through the curing process and is now ready to use is known as re-batched soap. Then, you grate it and heat it until it is gloopy and soft. You might now add a small amount of the infused oil before pouring the mixture into molds to re-harden.

How to Prepare Herb-Infused Oil for Cosmetics and Salve

Oil and herbs that are good for the skin are two of the most widely used substances in natural skincare. I use the term "oil" to refer to basic fats that are extracted from either plants or animals; examples are olive oil, lanolin, and sweet almond oil. Consider the botanicals that are frequently included in upscale skincare products when considering plants. While some of them are hard to find, others appear as plants or weeds in your garden or lawn. By learning to make herb-infused oils, you can use oil and skincare plants to create your own skincare products. Finding uses for oil in skin care is simple. Plants are a little trickier because there aren't many situations where you'd want to have plant matter on your skin! Instead, we can transfer their curative qualities into another substance, like oil. Herbal oil infusion is the best method because it's convenient and has a long shelf life. You can apply herb-infused oil straight to your skin or use it as a component in salves, creams, lotions, balms, ointments, and everyday skincare products.

Herbal Skin Care Oil

The skin can benefit greatly from plants on the inside as well as the outside. We can eat foods made of plants, and our bodies can use those nutrients to nourish our entire existence, including our skin. Additionally, you can directly apply plants that are high in chemicals that are good for the skin. That includes calendula flowers to purify and heal chickweed to calm, and comfrey leaf to promote healing.

Some plants have significant oil content that can be obtained through cold pressing or other techniques. It is frequently extremely simple to press and crush the plant to release this valuable oil. In the case of extra virgin olive oil, this is true. Many plant-based oils can assist in conditioning and sealing in moisture when they are applied to the skin. They frequently also possess skin-friendly qualities on their own.

We combine these oils, either made from plant or animal sources, with herbal material to make herb-infused oils. The plant's oil-soluble component infuses into the oil over time and with warmth, frequently changing the color of the oil. Through the carrier oil's soothing and conditioning properties as well as the herbal ingredient you add, this infused oil nourishes skin in two different ways.

Herbs for Salves and Skincare

Some plants and flowers can soothe, purify, energize, heal, and tighten your skin. It can be quite helpful to apply plant materials directly to our skin, such as aloe Vera for sunburns or face masks. Plantain is a leafy herb that grows on lawns and is one that I use directly on the skin. I will chew a leaf and apply the pulp to my skin if I feel an itch while in the garden. It offers quick relief! However, you may create herb-infused oil using a variety of herbs, including plantain, to use later. It helps keep their healing abilities intact for eventual use. When it's not possible or desirable to have leaf goop on your skin

Arnica, calendula, cannabis, chamomile, chickweed, comfrey, common daisies, echinacea, lavender, lemon balm, peppermint, plantain, rosemary, self-heal, St. John's wort, and yarrow are a few of the skincare herbs you can use to prepare an herb-infused oil. When producing herb-infused oil, it's typically better to work with dried herbs. You may dry cultivated herbs on a rack or in a food dehydrator set to a low temperature.

Solid and Liquid Oil Carrier Types

Please be aware that many different materials are referred to as "oil." For instance, cooking oil and oil for cars are very different. It's recommended to start by considering carrier oils in the same category as cooking oils when creating infused oils. They have an oily viscosity, are frequently edible, and should be safe to apply to your skin.

Sunflower oil and olive oil are common carrier oils for herb-infused oils, and the best oils are those that are physically pressed (squeezed) from sunflower seeds or olives. The oil releases a large portion of the plant's beneficial properties. When creating herb-infused oil, extra virgin, cold-pressed, or organic carrier oil is frequently the best option. It implies that the plant oil is the purest form of natural you can find.

Additionally, solid fats derived from plants or animals can be used to create infused oils. Others require heat and alternative processing, while some are pressed in the same manner as liquid oils. In either case, you must melt solid oils before using them to create infused oils so that the herbal material can interact with the oil.

You typically need to mix liquid oils with solid oils to make homemade salves. The mixture of the oils, when melted and cooled, produces a firmness that lies in between the consistency of the individual oils. Herbs used in skincare should be infused into some or all of the oils used to manufacture salves.

Herb-infused oil carrier oils for skincare

It's advisable to use just one of these oils each batch when creating herb-infused oil. You combine several oils when manufacturing salves and other skincare products. When buying carrier oils, try to find providers who also sell cosmetics. Oil purchased from the grocery store is frequently of lesser quality and has a shorter shelf life.

• Almond, apricot kernel, grape seed, jojoba, rice bran, safflower, and wheat germ liquid oils for facial skincare

• Almond, avocado, fractionated coconut, olive, rapeseed, rice bran, safflower, and sunflower oils are liquid oils for salves, lip, and body care. For all-purpose oil for infusing, a light-colored (as opposed to extra virgin) olive oil is the best option out of these. Even when heated a little warmer than is ideal, this oil is durable and lasts far longer than others do.

• Solid fats and butters, such as tallow, cocoa butter, lanolin, coconut oil, mango butter, Shea butter, and babassu. For use on the face, many of these are too heavy and pore-clogging. However, they can all be used to create salves for the body and lips.

Essential oils versus herbal oils

The organic substances needed to make herb-infused oils are made of glycerin and fatty acids. However, essential oil is not used to manufacture herb-infused oil.

Even though they are a different kind of oil and go by the same name, you wouldn't use them to infuse plants. Additionally, they differ from the infused oils that can be produced by macerating herbs in carrier oil.

Essential oils are a concentrated form of a plant's volatile oils, making them powerful for plant-based skin therapy. They don't have the same viscosity as carrier oils, they can't be used to infuse herbs, and most of them are dangerous to apply undiluted to the skin. They are included as an optional ingredient in the final phase to leave-on skincare products and ointments at a rate of 2% or less of the recipe (by weight).

Oil with Slow Herbal Infusion

Herbs are macerated in oil at room temperature to create herb-infused oil, which is the quickest and most popular method. All dried herbs for skin care that has oil-soluble components can be used with this technique.

Start with top-notch, thoroughly dried herbs that are ideally younger than a year old. You gain the advantage of knowing when they were collected and how they were dried if you grow your own. Additionally, bought herbs are frequently sold at a less fresh state, which could result in a decline in herbal quality. Three years is the normal shelf-life for purchased herbs, which is typically two years too long! From halfway to the top, loosely fill a jar with complete dried plant material. I suggest going all the way to the top if the plant stuff is fluffy and light. Halfway and more substantial, like lavender buds, is good. You can choose the jar's size based on your requirements.

I often create herb-infused oil in jars ranging from a jam jar to a quart in size.

You can add one or more herbs to a carrier oil to create a herb-infused oil for skin care. But for future reference, be sure to keep track of how much of each plant you used.

Then, drizzle the herbs with a single drop of your preferred liquid carrier oil. Fill the jar to within a half-inch of the top, cover it with a lid, and then store it somewhere cool and out of direct sunshine. Give the jar a little shake every few days or whenever you remember for the next four weeks. If you use dry herbs, it is irrelevant if they float to the surface of the oil. Since there is no water in the jar, it won't decay or grow mold.

Herbal Oil with a Solar Infusion

As an alternative, you can make the herb and oil jar according per the directions in the procedure above and then place the jar on a warm windowsill (70-80°F/21-27°C). However, sunlight's UV rays harm oil and can hasten oxidation and deterioration. The oil will be shielded from UV rays, kept warm, and the herbal properties of the plant material will be slowly extracted from the oil by enclosing the jar in a brown paper bag. After two weeks when kept in a warm location like a window sill, your herb-infused oil will be ready.

Making Herbal Oil using Fresh Herbs

Herb-infused oil can be made with either fresh or dried herbs, but there is a catch. Since dried herbs don't add moisture to the oil, they are much simpler and safer to utilize. Oil with water in it is more likely to oxidize, harbor germs, and go rancid. Additionally, dry herbs don't pose a threat to your oil's safety from botulism contamination, which is a concern if you're preparing lip salves. Do fresh herbs.

However, you can still prepare herb-infused oil with fresh herbs. Use fresh plant material wherever appropriate, such as with St. John's wort, mullein flowers, and chickweed. When using fresh, the idea is to either immediately infuse the material (as with the crockpot approach above) or make sure that it remains buried beneath the oil's surface. If you don't do this, the plant matter will rot, mold, and contaminate the oil with pathogens. When using wet herbs, such as chickweed, you should also let the leaves wilt for twelve hours before starting the infusion. During this time, turn the leaves over so that any remaining moisture can escape. I suggest using a fermentation weight to keep the plant material buried under the oil if you want to use fresh herbs in the slow-infused herbal oil process. Additionally, you must strain and decant the resulting oil in a very specific manner. Last but not least, never use lip cosmetics that contain herb-infused oils made with fresh herbs. They might be contaminated with botulism.

Method for Making Herb-Infused Oil in a Crockpot

Although there are various approaches, I usually employ the process for creating herb-infused oil. Many of us use crockpots, which are excellent kitchen appliances, to make stews, soups, and even hot-process soap. This technique can be used to infuse butters, solid oils, and liquid oils with herbs. The temperature will be warm but not scorching if your crockpot has a warm setting (not to be confused with low). Crockpots' low setting is sadly too hot to utilize for this technique. High temperatures can affect the chemical composition of oil and lead to oxidation. When creating herb-infused oil, you want to stay away from it, especially if you're utilizing cold-pressed oils. Just keep in mind that extreme temperatures, particularly high temperatures that last for a long time or repeatedly, can damage your oil.

Dried herbs should be placed in the crockpot dish, followed by your preferred carrier oil. Fill to completely enclose the herbs. The crockpot will then be put to the "warm" setting for an hour before being turned off. Before using the straining procedure described further down, repeat this the following day and the day after that.

Method for Making Herb-Infused Oil Using a Double Boiler

Use a double boiler to create herb-infused oil even more quickly. In an emergency, you can make one by nesting a stainless steel saucepan inside a bigger one. Water is poured into the bigger pot, which is then heated to a simmer. The smaller pan is heated in an indirect manner since it floats on this hot water. By using a double boiler, you can prevent the smaller pan's contents from being completely affected by the direct heat.

Use a double boiler and half-fill the smaller pan with herbs to create herb-infused oil. Next, totally cover them with oil by pouring it over them. With this technique, you can create herb-infused oil using either liquid or solid oil. In either case, the oil must completely cover the herbs. It might be necessary to wait for solid oils to melt before adding additional.

Place the smaller pan with the oil and herbs on top of the bigger pan with low-simmering water, and then heat everything through for one to two hours. During this time, maintain the temperature between 49 and 60 degrees Celsius (120 to 140 degrees Fahrenheit). Water can spurt up and into your oil pan if the water is simmered too vigorously.

Making Herb-Infused Oil with Alcohol

Oil is a great way to extract the medicinal elements of herbs, but it will only do so for oil-soluble components. The best solvent to use when trying to extract all of a plant's therapeutic qualities is alcohol. Additionally, it doesn't carry the hazards that adding water to herb-infused oil can.

One ounce (28 g) of dry plant material is pulsed to a powder using this technique. It should be combined with half an ounce (14 g) of high-proof brandy or vodka and macerated for a day. The following day, combine the herb-alcohol mixture with eight ounces (227 g) of liquid carrier oil in a blender. After that, you'll turn on your blender and give it five full minutes to blend. As stated below for all herb-infused oils, strain and store as necessary.

Straining Oil Infused with Herbs

Whichever of the aforementioned techniques you employed, you will strain and store infused oil in a similar manner. After the maceration period, strain the oil that has been infused with plant material using a sieve or other device to remove the plant matter. I frequently use a fine-mesh sieve over a bowl, lining it with cheesecloth as well. It is quick, and you can roll up the fabric and herbs and wring out any extra oil. By doing this, the majority of the herbal material in your gorgeous infused oil will be removed. The herbal material will then be placed back into the sieve, where I'll let any leftover oil drip out overnight. The herbs or flowers are then placed in the compost bin, and I thoroughly wash the cheesecloth by hand and in the washing machine. Your oil may still include some sediment even after this method of filtering. You may get rid of it by putting the herb-infused oil through a sieve packed with coffee filters. Simply place an everyday coffee filter inside a sieve over a basin. The oil passes through more slowly, and you will notice that the filter eventually clogs up. You must alter the filter if that occurs. You can also include any surplus oil that may have leaked overnight from the herbal material.

There is a further step you must take right now if you're using fresh herbs. The filtered oil should be put in a tall glass jar and left to settle for the night. The following day, carefully pour the oil from the top of the jar, discarding the lowest half-inch. The fresh herbs' added moisture will gradually sink to the bottom. The herb-infused oil can be distinguished from moisture that can introduce pathogens by removing the top layer of oil.

Keeping Herbal Oils Safe

Pour herb-infused oil into glass bottles; give them a date and content label. Keep them in a dark location if the glass is clear. As an alternative, you can store the oil in dark glass bottles. In the world of cosmetic packaging, brown and blue bottles are rather common. You can keep your oil on a shelf if it is kept in opaque bottles, but make sure to keep it out of the sun and out of the heat. Regarding shelf life, you should utilize your herb-infused oil either one year after making it or by the best-by date of the carrier oil you used.

What can you do with your prepared herbal oils now that they are ready? You can use infused oil to produce skincare products or apply it directly to the skin. Making homemade skincare products is a great place to start using herb-infused oils. This comprises salves, lip balm, massage oils, serums, eyelash oils, lotions, creams, and eyelash oils.

Benefits of Using Natural Skin Care Products over the Long Term

No negative effects.

The most delicate and important organ in our body is the skin. Protecting our skin from outside influences and avoiding doing it harm out of carelessness is the first step towards skin wellness. Since our species has co-evolved with nature, natural ingredients readily penetrate our skin, in contrast to the complicated artificial compounds that are included in the majority of skincare products. As a result, our skin reacts unfavorably and develops rashes, redness, acne, and other conditions. When used over an extended period of time, skincare products composed of pure, natural ingredients produce astonishing results without the worry of experiencing any negative side effects or allergies.

Skin Glow and Radiant Skin

There are countless treasures in nature for people. And using skincare products with natural components helps us get the flawless skin we all desire. Because these substances adhere to the same standards as organic food, this is made feasible. Therefore, there are no complex chemicals, no synthetic formulations, and no artificial aroma. Instead, effective natural components like aloe Vera, hydrogenated castor oil (castor wax), pharmaceutical-grade castor oil, coconut oil, turmeric, sandalwood, rose water, etc. are used to make natural skincare products. By including these components into our regular skincare regimen, we are able to get rid of all skin problems and get glowing, healthy skin.

Defends Against Premature Skin Aging

Skin aging and deterioration as we age are both natural processes. Premature skin aging, however, is a serious warning sign that can indicate serious underlying illnesses. Therefore, it is crucial and required to take immediate action to avoid premature skin aging. Although there are many products on the market to combat skin aging, and some of them do work, they also include a lot of hazardous and damaging ingredients. Instead of exposing our skin to potentially harmful ingredients, natural skincare products function more harmoniously with our bodies to reduce premature aging. Among many other possibilities, quinoa face packs and jojoba oil have been proven to be quite helpful in preventing premature skin aging.

Enhances general health and wellbeing

We don't hesitate to use the newest, "cooler" skin care product that everyone is raving about. But if we just flip the product package over, read the ingredients, and then research the qualities of those compounds online, we're probably in for the shock of our lives. The majority of cosmetics and skin care products contain substances like sodium lauryl sulfate, phthalates, and parabens. These substances have the potential to harm our immune, reproductive, and endocrine systems as well as our general health. Utilizing natural skin care products does not compromise our overall health and, in fact, enhances it because the body interprets natural substances as food. Additionally, natural substances promote cell regeneration, enhance moisture retention, and have no detrimental effects on the immune system.

Real sustainability

Natural skin care products use only substances that have been taken directly from the environment. As a result, natural skin care products are easily biodegradable when it comes to disposal. Additionally, because these products generate less trash, disposal is made simpler. Natural skin care products are also cruelty-free because they are not tested on animals before being released for human consumption.

By choosing natural skin care products, we have the opportunity to heal our bodies and the environment through our conscious choices.

Switching to natural skin care products appears perfect for both the environment and for us as humans. And while utilizing natural skin care products may first seem like an expensive change to undertake financially, over time, these advantages will far outweigh any costs in a significant way.

How to verify a genuine Organic Skincare Product

Cosmetics that are counterfeit are becoming a serious issue. How then do we distinguish between them? A substantial likelihood of the product being a fake exists if it does not come directly from an authorized vendor or manufacturer.

Here are some pointers you might bear in mind when you're out shopping and intend to purchase a natural cosmetic product:

Check the Label Specifically:

Important information on the packaging is frequently cleverly omitted by counterfeit goods. Pay attention to the following red flags: misspelled words, mistakes, and subpar printing. All should undergo thorough inspection. To ensure that everything matches up with the packing, double check the product on the official website of the company.

Take a look at the first five components:

The next step is to scan the packaging for the first five ingredients listed. The brands must list their constituents in the order of their highest to lowest concentrations, according the rules. The majority of the product is typically made up of the first five ingredients. The first five should be checked first, then if you have time, go over the full ingredient list.

Consider avoiding these components:

You can also keep an eye out for ingredients that you ought to be aware of and think about avoiding. We have compiled a comprehensive guide to help you better understand what to avoid.

• Sulphates:

These are the kinds of detergents that are frequently present in cleaning supplies. These can deplete the natural moisture in skin and weaken its protective barrier because they are so harsh on the body. They might aggravate you and make you feel even dryer. Search for words that include the word "sulphate" in their name, such as sodium laureth sulphate.

• Silicones:

These stop pores from absorbing substances and interfering with the skin's natural processes. These might worsen dehydration if used frequently and can possibly encourage acne. Watch out for words that end in "-cone," "-conol," or "-siloxane."

•Petroleum oil

Kerosene in the deodorized form is known as mineral oil. It can disrupt the process of cell renewal, encourage acne, and worsen dryness due to its occlusive nature that affects the skin.

• Artificial Fragrance

When using the product, they are the main cause of allergic skin reactions. The phrase is also used to refer to phthalates and covert substances. Phthalates have been related to issues like disrupted hormone production. Look for wording on the package that contain words like "parfum" or "fragrance." Try to stay away from fragrance-free goods because they frequently suggest the use of masking ingredients.

•Polyunsaturated fatty acids (PUFAs)

The fatty acid chains of these oils have several unsaturated double bonds. They are unstable and prone to attack by free radicals. It oxidizes, commonly known as pro-aging, when it is exposed to oxygen. Sunflower, sesame, soybean, and rose hip oils are a few of the popular oils that contain PUFAs. When using oils that contain more than 10% PUFA, try to keep your distance.

• Parabens:

Preservatives known as "parabens" are a term that we have all come across. However, the fact that they mimic estrogen is the reason we must avoid the same. Look for words that finish in "-paraben." Many firms have switched from paraben to phenoxyethanol, which although somewhat safer, is nonetheless unpleasant.

- Chemical sunblock

Organic sunscreen is another name for chemical sunscreen. The ingredients, however, are entirely synthetic because they are laden with toxins. Oxybenzone, octisalate, homosalate, octinoxate, and octocrylene make up the majority of common sunscreen ingredients. In order to determine if a sunscreen contains chemicals or not, people most frequently look for zinc oxide and titanium dioxide. If these are missing from the ingredient list, the sunscreen is chemical.

Checking the labels and taking your time when reading the ingredient list is an excellent habit to get into whenever you are out shopping for new products. You'll be able to choose better options thanks to this.

Chapter 2

Hair Growth and Maintenance Herbs

Many men and women worry about their hair loss. Your hair loss could be caused by a variety of factors, including hormone fluctuations, vitamin deficiencies, and heredity. Hair loss or thinning may also be brought on by certain medical diseases, such as thyroid illness.

Although there is no miracle treatment for hair growth, several herbs may help to halt hair loss or encourage new growth. However, it's crucial to remember that, especially if your hair loss is brought on by a medical condition, you should consult your doctor before incorporating herbs into your daily regimen.

Taking good care of your hair is essential for maintaining its health and preventing serious damage that can result in hair loss.

Regular washing using shampoos and conditioners endorsed by celebrities is insufficient. You should know how to take daily care of your hair if you want it to be strong, healthy, and lustrous.

For both men and women, taking care of their hair is a crucial aspect of good hygiene. Nobody wants to leave the house with frizzy, unhealthy hair. Hair care also entails good grooming and ensuring you are using the right products; simply washing your hair doesn't always guarantee you've done it correctly.

Depending on the weather and what you do during the day, you should wash your hair more frequently. Your hair needs to be washed more frequently if it becomes oily rapidly. Straight hair can easily become greasy. Very curly hair requires fewer washes because it is less greasy. If your hair is thick, curly, or kinky, it may be too dry and appear frizzy. Even if using a conditioner after washing your hair could be helpful, it won't make your hair healthier. Bear in mind that conditioner might improve the appearance of already-dead hair.

Hair classification

There are two widely used methods for identifying your hair type.

As follows is the Andre Walker system:

Type 1: Straight hair

Type 2: Wavy hair

Type 3: Curly hair

Type 4: Kinky hair

Straight Hair

Straight hair lies flat from the roots to the ends and is difficult to curl. Typically, it is silky and velvety. Women with this hair type frequently have oily scalps, which contributes to the uniform greasiness of their hair.

Wavy Hair

This hairstyle falls in between curly and straight. As it moves from the roots to the ends, you could see lovely, large curls. The texture of this hair type is often coarse. It holds hairstyles firmly. Because of this, this hair type is the most practical and the simplest to experiment with if you want to straighten, curl, or style your hair in any way.

Curly Hair

The pronounced curls that extend from the roots down define this hair type. Compared to straight and wavy hair, curly hair is more prone to being dry and frizzy.

Further classifications for curly hair include:

- Type 3A (loose curls)
- Type 3B (medium curls)
- Type 3C (tight curls)

Kinky Hair

This hair type, also referred to as "African American" hair, is characterized by extremely tight curls and is particularly delicate. If improper care is not taken, it can shatter easily.

Kinky hair can also be divided into:

- Type 4A (soft)
- Type 4B (wiry)
- Type 4C (extremely wiry)

You can further categorize your hair type depending on luster, thickness, and texture once you've decided which of the four groups you fall into. The L.O.I.S system, which classifies hair based on curl pattern, is the second hair type method.

L- Hair has zigzag bends at acute angles.

O- Hair forms circles or ringlets by curling on itself.

I- Hair is flat and lacks a recognizable curl pattern.

S- The hair is styled in waves.

In addition to assigning your hair a letter type, the L.O.I.S system categorizes texture as

1. Thready

2. Wiry

3. Cottony

4. Spongy

5. Silky

It is up to you to decide which classification system to adopt if your head has any variant or mix of the aforementioned hair kinds.

Herbs for hair

Gingko Biloba

This herb is known to increase circulation and blood flow. It can aid in boosting the blood flow that follicles require to promote new root growth. Although it can be used topically, it is most frequently consumed as a tea since, like most herbs; the benefits are obtained through digestion. It is notably beneficial for persons with follicle-related deficits and is also available as a supplement. This herb promotes "hair regeneration, through simultaneous actions on proliferation and death of the cells in the hair follicle, thereby showing potential as a hair tonic," according to research.

Rosemary

This herb is frequently used as oil, either by itself or in combination with olive oil to promote growth. It also has the added benefit of preventing early graying. Additionally, it is incredibly hydrating, making it useful for treating a dry, flaky scalp that can prevent new growth. According to a study discovered in the Phototherapy Research Journal, applying rosemary topically to mice improved hair growth by preventing the creation of too much testosterone.

Peppermint

Another herb that brings healing to the scalp and promotes growth is peppermint. It hydrates and calms an inflamed scalp while also igniting the hair follicles. Don't undervalue herbs that just function to repair the scalp as a way of development because a healthy scalp is the foundation of hair growth. This plant can be taken as tea or is frequently used as oil applied directly to the scalp or as an ingredient in hair products. A Toxicological Research on the use of peppermint oil for hair growth revealed that 92% of patients had hair growth at the end of four weeks.

Aloe Vera

This plant's gel is frequently utilized in hair products. The gel can assist the scalp's pH equilibrium be restored, which promotes growth.

Since it is so moisturizing, it is also a terrific technique to hydrate and define your hair. For optimum results, rub this gel directly into the scalp. You can also make an aloe Vera rinse. Aloe Vera gel is used traditionally for hair loss and for improvement in hair development following alopecia.

Horsetail

This is one of the herbs that is less well known but is one of the ones that are used the most in hair products. Due to the presence of the component silica, it is known to strengthen bones and hair. It also aids in retaining hair by making it less brittle, which is beneficial for hair loss. It can be utilized in products that already include it as an ingredient or taken as a supplement. If used orally, this plant should be taken with plenty of water because it is a diuretic.

Lavender

Due to the antimicrobial qualities of this well-known plant, the scalp will be free of any impediments to growth. It will be nearly hard for growth to occur if your scalp is infested with a lot of parasites, fungus, or other undesirable elements. Although it can also be prepared into a tea, this herb is frequently applied topically in the form of oil. Many hair care companies also include lavender in their products.

Burdock

Burdock helps soothe an itchy scalp and stop hair loss since it is rich in phytosterol components and necessary fatty acids. Because of these two components, it can aid in stimulating new growth and is frequently present in hair care products meant to revive hair. In fact, psoriasis can be treated using the fatty acids found in this plant. According to the University of Maryland Medical Center, in a trial of 40 psoriasis patients, those who combined their prescription treatments with fish oil rich in the same fatty acids found in burdock saw better benefits than those who took only their medication.

Stinging Nettle

This herb aids in preventing excessive DHT production, which causes hair loss. It may not stimulate new growth, but it does reduce hair loss and aid in reestablishing the proper balance of hormones that stimulate hair growth. Additionally, it possesses potent antimicrobial qualities. This outcome may be linked to the presence of agglutinin, a lectin, and other active chemicals in the plant.

Ginseng

This plant, which is also frequently used in hair care products, is known to promote the circulation necessary for hair growth. Additionally, it can strengthen hair strands to aid in hair retention. According to a study, ginseng extracts help hair follicles grow back in a healthy way.

Zee Palmetto

This herb, which is related to stinging nettle, works to prevent the hormonal imbalance that inhibits growth. In fact, combining the two as a topical will yield the best benefits in terms of halting hair loss and promoting growth. Additionally, it reduces the overproduction of DHT. By preventing DHT from attaching to receptors, saw palmetto extract prevents DHT from acting and speeds up the degradation of the powerful molecule.

Organic hair oils

Herbal extracts are combined with a carrier oil basis to create hair oils, commonly known as hair tonics. Various herbs and carrier oils are used in some hair oils.

The following popular carrier oils are used to create herbal oils:

- Cocoa butter
- Sweet Almond oil
- Nutmeg oil
- Olive oil
- mineral oil
- Jojoba oil
- Wheat germ emulsion

Herbal hair oils made from certain botanicals include:

The Chinese hibiscus, also known as Hibiscus rosa sinensis, is an evergreen shrub. Tea made with its colorful, eatable blooms is made frequently. In order to stimulate hair follicles, improve follicle size, and promote hair growth, hibiscus is regarded to be beneficial.

- Bacopa monnieri, popularly known as brahmi: Brahmi is a creeping herb used in Ayurvedic medicine. It has alkaloids that are believed to trigger the proteins necessary for hair development.

• Coat buttons (Tridax procumbent): Coat buttons is a daisy-family plant that creeps and is used in Ayurvedic medicine. It has antioxidants and both on its own and when combined with other herbs, it stimulates hair growth.

• Jatamansi (Nardostachys jatamansi): This little shrub's rhizomes have been shown to hasten hair development. It has been demonstrated to promote hair development in chemotherapy-induced alopecia.

• Panax ginseng, sometimes known as ginseng, is a traditional natural medicine for a variety of ailments, including hair loss. It has saponins, which are thought to promote hair growth by preventing the activity of 5a reductase. This enzyme is connected to male pattern baldness.

Be sure to follow the manufacturer's recommendations because certain hair oils are designed to be used as a wash or a leave-in hair treatment. Whether to apply to damp or dry hair is specified on the product.

Massage the hair oil into your scalp with clean fingertips, then rinse as advised.

Multi-herbal creams

Herbal ointments, also known as herbal salves, are often created by mixing herbs with water, oil such as lanolin or petroleum jelly, and other ingredients. Beeswax or cocoa butter may be included as additional components. Most polyherbal ointments include a variety of herbal extracts.

In polyherbal ointments, certain herbs include:

•Gooseberry, or Emblica officinalis, is a common Ayurvedic plant. It's used to make hair stronger and encourage hair development. Additionally, it is reported to contain a number of antioxidants.

• Centella asiatica, sometimes known as gotu kola, is one of the most well-known Ayurvedic plants. It is believed to lengthen hair and encourage hair growth, perhaps via improving blood flow to the scalp.

• Aloe vera (A. Barbadensis Mill.): This tropical plant is used as a common folk treatment for digestive issues and burns. Additionally, it can be used to maintain a healthy, conditioned scalp, which can promote strong hair development.

•Holy basil (Ocimum sanctum) is a fragrant herb with adaptogenic qualities that is well-known for its therapeutic benefits. It might assist in preventing hair loss brought on by hormonal fluctuations, dandruff, itching, or both.

Typically, you apply polyherbal ointments straight to your scalp. As directed by the manufacturer, massage the ointment into your scalp with clean fingertips until it is fully absorbed.

Natural creams

Herbal oils and water are often utilized to make herbal creams. Compared to herbal ointments, they have less oil and more water, and your skin may readily absorb them.

Herbal creams may contain the following herbs:

• Giant dodder (Cuscuta reflexa Roxb): By blocking the 5a reductase enzyme, giant dodder, an expansive Ayurvedic herb, is said to help treat alopecia brought on by steroid hormones.

• Bitter apple (Citrullus colocynthis): Ayurveda uses the fruit of the bitter apple plant, which grows in the desert. To treat hair loss, its dried fruit pulp is employed. Glycosides, which are substances thought to start hair growth, are present in bitter apples.

• False Daisy (Eclipta alba): In Ayurveda, false daisy is a herb that promotes hair development. False daisy causes a faster stage of hair growth in mice by stimulating the hair follicles.

• Night-flowering jasmine (Nyctanthes arbortristis): This little flowering plant is Originally from South Asia. Research has shown that night-flowering jasmine stimulated rat hair growth and may be useful in treating alopecia.

Apply the hair cream to your hair from roots to tips or massage it into your scalp with clean hands, as directed by the manufacturer.

Natural gels

Herbal extracts are combined with a gel base in herbal gels. Typically, they don't have oil in them. Herbal gels that support healthy hair may contain the following herbs:

• Trigonella foenum-graecum, also known as fenugreek: this plant belongs to the pea family. It's a well-liked seasoning with possible hair-growth advantages. Fenugreek seed extract, according to studies, increased hair volume and thickness in men and women who had mild hair loss.

• Marking nut (Semecarpus anacardium), a plant from the sub-Himalayan region that promotes hair growth in Ayurvedic and Siddha therapy. To ascertain the efficacy and safety of marking nuts, more study is required.

Using clean hands massage the gel into your scalp or apply to your hair from roots to tips as per manufacturer's directions.

Cubosomes suspensions

Cubosomes are crystalline nanoparticles that are liquid. Drugs and, in some situations, herbal medicines are delivered with the help of cubosomal suspensions.

Herbs like these can be found in cubosomal suspensions for hair growth:

• Oriental arborvitae (Thuja orientalis): A tree belonging to the cypress family, Oriental arborvitae is an evergreen. It is an age-old treatment for baldness. The herb promotes the development phase in dormant hair follicles, which aids in hair growth.

•Mexico is the country where espinosilla (Loeselia mexicana) is grown. It helps keep the scalp healthy and works to strengthen hair follicles. A study found that male mice treated with espinosilla had some hair growth.

• Goji berry (Lycium chinense Mill): In traditional Chinese medicine, this fruit-bearing shrub is used to encourage hair development. Zinc, which is present in goji berries, is thought to help the scalp produce oil, preventing dandruff, which can result in hair loss.

• Tuber fleeceflower (Polygonum multiflorum): This tuber is a common treatment for hair loss in traditional Chinese medicine. It comprises substances that prevent 5a reductase enzyme activity. Additionally, it aids in promoting the hair follicles' growth stage.

Apply or comb through your hair from root to tip with clean hands, or as otherwise directed. Use herbal cubosomal suspensions as your physician has prescribed.

Potential negative consequences and dangers

Allergic reaction is the biggest risk associated with herbal hair growth products. Before using any herbs, you should always perform a patch test to check for an adverse reaction.

How to do it:

1. Use a little product and rub it into your wrist.

2. Keep on for at least a day.

3. You can apply it elsewhere if you don't notice any irritation after a day.

If you do encounter an allergic response, you can go through

- Rash

- hives

- Redness
- itching
- Having trouble breathing
- Dizziness
- Headache

The following are possible negative effects of topical herbal hair growth products:

- Hair thinning
- More hair falling out
- Dry head
- Redness or inflammation of the scalp

Most herbs for hair growth have unsearched adverse effects in humans. It would be impossible to standardize dosing advice without more data.

Women who are expecting or nursing shouldn't use herbs to grow hair unless a doctor or certified natural health practitioner is present to supervise them. A whole head of hair cannot be grown with a herbal cure. Herbal products that promise to stimulate hair growth should be avoided. Some herbs may support healthy scalps, thicken hair, strengthen hair, or speed up the hair growth cycle, according to research. Even yet, more human clinical trials are required before herbal medicines are used as a standard method of hair growth.

When to visit a doctor if your hair is thinning

Even though it's normal to lose hair during the day, if you're losing more than 100 hairs every day, you should talk to your doctor. Additionally, you should consult your doctor if you have concerns about ongoing hair loss, a receding hairline, or if you suddenly notice patchy hair loss. Patches of hair loss could be an indication of a serious illness.

Frequently asked questions regarding hair thinning.

What leads to hair thinning?

Your hair loss could be brought on by a variety of lifestyle choices, genetics, recent life events (such as giving birth or losing a lot of weight quickly), or medical disorders. Specific hair products, tight hairstyles, high stress levels, and a deficiency in certain vitamins and minerals in the diet can all be considered lifestyle issues. A weakened immune system may also cause hair thinning in some individuals.

Can hair that is thinning regrow?

Thinning hair may regrow depending on what caused the hair to thin in the first place. Regrowth of hair may be experienced by people whose hair is thinning because of vitamin deficiencies, stress, pregnancy, or other non-genetic causes. It is important to see your doctor if you notice any new hair loss or thinning.

Thinning hair may be a symptom of several medical disorders.

Why is my hair thinning out of nowhere?

Numerous factors, including a time of intense stress, pregnancy, stopping the use of birth control pills, hormonal changes, a high fever, or yanking at your hair, might result in sudden hair thinning. Hair loss in clumps or sudden, persistent hair thinning may indicate an underlying medical issue. Consult your doctor if this happens.

Which shampoo should I use if my hair is thinning?

You might need to go through a period of trial and error to locate the shampoo that works best for you because hair loss can occur for a variety of reasons. While some shampoos work to stop hair loss, others thicken already existing hair. You can also discuss prescription-strength shampoo for thinning hair with your physician. While hair thinning can initially be unsettling, many different types of thinning hair are curable.

You should consult a doctor if you notice any new hair loss or thinning, or if you start to develop any bald spots. They can provide you with any necessary medications as well as assist you in identifying any underlying medical concerns.

Another treatment option for severe alopecia might be hair transplants.

Hair care

How Frequently You Should Wash Your Hair; Different Factors influencing it

It's not advised to wash your hair every day. Shampoos strip your hair of the moisture and essential oils it needs to stay hydrated. You should only think about washing your hair with shampoo frequently if you fall into one of the following categories:

Oily hair

Dirt and pollution are more likely to stick to oily hair. This might cause clogged pores and the emergence of other ailments like dandruff. How oily your scalp is depends on your age, genes, way of life, and hormonal changes. If your scalp is particularly greasy for any of these reasons, you might need to wash your hair almost every day.

Type 2 hair

The straighter your hair is, the greasier it will be. Compared to textured or curly hair, fine, straight hair needs to be washed more frequently.

Pollen or dust grains

If you spend a lot of time gardening or working outside, you may need to wash your hair more frequently because your scalp is exposed to more dust and pollution.

Way of living

Your scalp may feel sweatier and require washing every one to two days if you travel frequently or exercise frequently.

Hair care regimen based on your hair type

Straight hair

Most of us have a tendency to believe that straight hair is simple to care for and does not require a strict regimen. Straight hair, on the other hand, is something that becomes greasy easily and requires the same level of maintenance as the other hair.

How to Wash:

•Use a sulfate-free shampoo to help you remove extra grease and grime from your hair. Products that are designed specifically to help prevent oil and grease on your scalp are available.

• Unless your scalp is excessively greasy for another reason, washing your hair once every two to three days is advised.

• Use a mild conditioner instead of a leave-in one. They could make your hair feel overly heavy and droopy.

•Even better, choose a conditioner that includes oils like coconut or jojoba oil. Without weighting it down, this will keep your hair healthy and silky.

•Don't condition your roots; simply use conditioner on your shaft. By doing this, it won't taste overly fatty and won't fall flat.

•Your hair won't become flat at the roots if you use a volumizing mousse. Before letting it dry, apply it to damp hair.

Wavy Hair

If cared for, wavy hair can be greatly experimented with. This hair type lies in the between of straight and curly hair, making styling it simple.

How to Wash:

•Because it tends to be drier than straight hair, wavy hair doesn't require as frequent washing. Once every 3–4 days is recommended for washing wavy hair.

•For you, using a shampoo made especially for wavy hair types without sulfates should work.

• You can keep your hair nourished and healthy by massaging some oil into it before washing. This can be done an hour before to washing your hair.

•Every time you wash your hair, condition it.

Any plant may be utilized in the formulation of a herbal hair product. However, it could be challenging to locate over-the-counter hair growth products that contain the study's botanicals. You might be able to locate the treatment that best fits your needs with the assistance of your doctor or a natural health professional. Before using it, be sure to consult your doctor. They can explain your treatment options to you and give you guidance on any subsequent actions.

•Wavy hair's ends tend to be drier than straight hair's. To avoid this and keep the shaft and ends of your hair moisturized, use oil.

• To scrunch your hair and highlight those waves, you can even use a leave-in conditioner. When you get out of the shower, apply it to moist hair and bend your hair forward. To give it bounce, scrunch your hair with your fists and let it air dry.

Curly Hair

Your personality is given a sense of fun and life by having curly hair. However, it is challenging to maintain and prone to drying out quickly.

How to Wash:

- Use a shampoo that does not contain sulphur to wash your hair. Only wash your scalp with shampoo because that is what has to be cleaned. If used on the shaft, shampoos have a tendency to eliminate moisture and essential oils, which can cause your hair to become overly dry and frizzy.

- To keep it from getting too dry, only wash your hair once a week.

- You can maintain your hair silky and moisturized by applying conditioner every three to four days.

- Conditioning is more crucial to hair health than shampooing. This keeps the hair healthy and frizz-free. To prevent your scalp and hair from becoming dry, you can even mix a few drops of an essential oil into your conditioner. Your regimen may include deep-conditioning your hair on a regular basis.

• After using conditioner, detangle your hair in the shower. This is the best defense against it breaking.

• To make those loops shine out, use a curl-defining cream!

• To avoid frizzy hair, get a diffuser attachment. With the aid of these appliances, you may dry your hair in a specific pattern and avoid frizz.

Kinky Hair

Very tight curls are the defining feature of this hair type. It frequently has a relatively dry climate.

How to Wash:

• To keep your hair from becoming very dry, use a gentle sulfate-free shampoo.

• Pay attention to the rhizomes and stay away from the shafts. Your hair's natural oils are frequently removed by shampoos.

•Every two to three days during the week, you can co-wash with a conditioner.

• Deep-condition your hair at least once a week to replenish its moisture and nutrients. It won't become dry and frizzy as a result of this.

• To keep your hair soft and hydrated, spritz a moisturizing formula on it each day.

•One hour before shampooing and conditioning it, oil your hair.

• After conditioning it, detangle your hair in the shower. This will avoid breaking.

Tips That Apply To All Hair Types

Oil Massage

To provide your hair nourishment and hydration, oiling it once a week is crucial. Even for your particular hair problems, you can use essential oils.

Ways to Massage:

• Blend your preferred carrier oil with an essential oil.

•Apply a warm paste on your scalp.

• For five minutes, gently massage the oil into your scalp. Then, let it on for around an hour.

• Shampoo and lukewarm water should be used to rinse.

Trim Your Hair

No, thinning your hair won't make it grow more quickly! However, it can help you by giving your hair a healthier, softer, and split-end-free appearance. Every two to three months, trimming is advised.

Try not to tie your hair up too frequently

Tying your hair up can lead to damage and eventually hair loss. This occurs as a result of the roots being yanked out repeatedly, which finally leads to their breaking.

Cover your hair When You Leave the House

Although it is well known that the sun may harm your skin, it can also dry out and harm your hair! In addition, smog and debris can build up on your scalp, making it unclean. Your hair may end up getting washed too frequently as a result, which could be detrimental over time.

Use Lukewarm or Cool Water to Wash Your Hair

Essential oils and moisture from the scalp are frequently stripped away by hot water. Rinse your hair with lukewarm or cool water.

Refrain from utilizing items that generate excessive heat

Your hair can be damaged by heat-producing product, which eventually leads to breakage and makes it look dry, lifeless, and frizzy. Apply a heat protectant as soon as you use a product like this to lessen harm. For your hair to be nourished, soft, and healthy, it's crucial to follow a hair care program tailored to your hair type. This also stops hair from breaking and falling out. How often you go outside, how oily your hair is, and your lifestyle all affect how frequently you wash your hair.

Be aware of the nature of your scalp or hair; make a point of massaging your hair with oil at least once a week. Your hair is strengthened and your follicles are helped by this in terms of nutrition. If you have any scalp issues that call for the use of medicated shampoos, stick to the treatment plan that your doctor has prescribed.

How to Prevent Hair Thinning

50 to 100 hairs are typically lost every day. Any more than this can indicate that you're losing hair more frequently than is healthy, which could lead to general hair thinning.

In contrast to widespread hair loss, thinning hair is not always associated with baldness. However, it does give the impression that you have bald patches on your head.

Typical lifestyle choices include:

• Excessive hair care. This covers relaxers, perms, and color treatments.

• Applying damaging hair products. Extreme-hold hair gels and sprays fall under this category.

• Donning tight hairdos. Wearing an up do or pulling your hair back into a ponytail while working out can pull on your hair and cause it to separate from the follicles, eventually resulting in thin areas.

• Consuming inadequate amounts of iron, folic acid, and other minerals. All of these support follicles' natural hair growth.

• Suffering from ongoing stress. An increase in hormones like cortisol is linked to stress. A surplus of stress hormones may prevent the growth of new hair.

Additionally, thinning hair may be inherited or result from underlying medical issues. If any of the following applies to you:

• Just had a baby.

•Stopped using birth control pills recently.

• experience hormonal changes

•Weight loss.

•Autoimmune condition.

• have deficits in the immune system

• suffer from a skin condition or infection

• lacking in vitamin D

Less frequently, thinning hair could be brought on by:

• ripping your own hair out

•Eating problems

• A severe fever

Home cures and treatments

Hair thinning may be addressed in some cases at home. The choices listed below are worth thinking about, but consult your doctor first.

A head massage

Scalp massage is arguably the least expensive way to try to grow your hair out fuller. It doesn't cost anything, and when done properly, it has no negative effects.

Use your fingertips to gently push down on your scalp while washing your hair to promote blood flow. Try using a handheld scalp massager to also exfoliate dead skin cells for even additional advantages.

Herbal extracts

Essential oils, which are liquids made from specific plants, are mostly utilized in aromatherapy and other forms of complementary treatment.

Some individuals who suffer from pattern baldness have utilized lavender oil successfully. Lavender is frequently mixed with other oils, like those derived from thyme and rosemary. Make sure to dilute your essential oil in carrier oil if you decide to try this treatment.

To see if there is a reaction, test a small bit of the oil on your arm and wait 24 hours. An allergic reaction may be indicated by hives, a rash, or other signs of redness or irritation.

Thinning hair shampoo

Two mechanisms are used by anti-thinning shampoos. These products firstly give your hair volume so that it seems fuller. Those who have thinning or naturally fine hair may find this useful.

In order to support a healthier scalp, shampoos for hair loss or thinning hair also include vitamins and amino acids. Use these products as instructed for the greatest results.

Multivitamins

Your general health affects your ability to maintain healthy hair. Malnutrition and several eating disorders can cause follicles to stop producing new hair. If you think you might be lacking in certain nutrients, a blood test can help. Your doctor could advise taking a daily multivitamin if you are deficient in a number of important nutrients. For healthy hair to continue growing thick and strong, it needs iron, folic acid, and zinc. Look for daily vitamins that fit these requirements for both men and women. If you are currently obtaining the nutrients you require, you should refrain from taking any additional vitamins. There is no proof that doing so will stop hair loss, and consuming too much of some nutrients may have the opposite effect.

Supplements with folic acid

A form of B vitamin called folic acid is crucial for the development of new cells. There is evidence from a few studies that some types of hair loss may be related to folate deficiencies. But much like with multivitamins, there isn't enough proof to say that folic acid will definitely contribute to thicker hair.

Biotin

Water-soluble vitamin B-7, or biotin, is naturally present in foods including liver, nuts, and lentils. It's unlikely that you have a biotin deficiency if you maintain a healthy diet. However, the popularity of supplemental biotin has increased recently, in part because of advertisements that highlighted how these pills will provide consumers more energy and greater hair growth. There is little proof that biotin can treat thinning hair, despite the fact that it aids in the breakdown of enzymes in your body. If you take vitamin B-5 supplements, avoid taking biotin. Together, they may lessen one another's effectiveness.

Chapter 3

Herbs for steaming

The Sacred Origin of Yoni Steam, the Herbs, and How to Steam

Yoni steaming is a potent, age-old form of self-care that women use all around the world to support their overall wellness, feminine power, and women's wisdom. Yoni steams, also known as V steams, pelvic steams, chai-yok, or bajo's, are a type of traditional feminine healing arts that are regaining popularity. Yoni steams, a comprehensive form of self-care, include a woman allowing the gentle warmth of herbal steam to permeate the outside of her vagina.

Yoni steams, which are a Maya therapeutic tradition, are primarily used to thoroughly clean the uterus after childbirth, throughout menopause, and when there are monthly problems. They are widely used by women in

Korea, Central America, India, and Eastern Europe as a part of their self-care regimens.

According to studies, simply being nicer, gentler, and more loving to ourselves can help us maintain good heart health. Depending on how much we love ourselves, our physiology can alter. I firmly believe that this is true for every part of our body, particularly the feminine and reproductive systems. Based on how we treat and value our bodies, we can increase the health of our vagina. The female genitalia, the womb, and the vagina are all referred to as yoni in Sanskrit. Its meaning of "sacred spot" alludes to our divine nature and its holy doorway to life.

The terms "golden lotus," "gates of heaven," "precious pearl," and "treasure" are used in ancient Taoist tradition to describe it. The vagina is the muscular tube in women and the majority of female mammals that connects the external genitalia to the cervix of the uterus.

The Latin root of the term "vagina" means "scabbard or sheath," a scabbard into which a sword might be slid. In the case of the anatomic vagina, the penis served as the "sword."

Google searches for other definitions turn up:

• The cause of life.

• "p*ssy," "down there," "cat," "goodness" a portal, etc.

• Even the most tenacious guys are susceptible to addiction

• A means by which women manipulate men and compel them to comply with their irrational demands

• A man only fully feels at home there.

• The only aspect of life that is worthwhile

Did you pay attention to your body's sensations while you read the descriptions? Some of them made you laugh, while others caused you to become distant. Here is an illustration of what

I'm trying to say. Our perception of our bodies affects how we feel. Our body's functionality is influenced by how we feel and how we talk about it.

Yoni steam

In a holistic health procedure known as a yoni steam, a lady lets warm herbal steam softly permeate the outside of her vagina. The vagina endures a lot between menstruation, sexual activity, and childbirth. Changing hormones, pelvic floor problems, and other factors might make the vaginal area uncomfortable at times. That is why yoni steaming, an old custom, is making a comeback. Basically, you or your open-backed chair sits underneath a steam kettle that is used to boil herbs. To create a sort of sweat lodge for your lower torso, blankets and sheets are wrapped around your body. As you sit, you take in the steam's velvety warmth. It directly enters your body through your yoni and travels up through a deep inner channel that connects to your heart to your uterus, pelvis, and even higher so you can feel better in your body and in life.

Benefits of yoni steams

The advantages of yoni steams are numerous. Here, I'll list them all and go into further detail about a handful of them that I believe are crucial.

- Control menstrual cycles that are erratic, lessen painful periods, bloating, and fatigue related to menstruation

- Diminish dark purple or brown blood and menstrual flow when menses first begin.

- Might increase fertility

- Postpartum recovery by helping to heal scars from C-sections, episiotomies, or vaginal tears

- Intercourse discomfort

- Recover from psychological or sexual abuse

- Reduce endometriosis, ovarian cysts, uterine prolapse and weakening, and uterine fibroids.

- Promote the recovery of hemorrhoids
- Treat UTIs and persistent yeast infections
- Reduce menopausal symptoms like discomfort or dryness during sex
- Cleanse the body of pollutants and detoxify the womb
- Let go of pent-up emotions
- More intense and frequent orgasms
- Use our creativity for projects, artwork, services, and soul-searching
- Boost libido & rekindle sensuous lust
- Strengthen your bond with your feminine side.
- A self-love and self-care action

Let's explore some of these points in more detail, including how frequently you ought to steam.

- Regular cycles: For individuals, who experience healthy, pain-free periods, I advise a seasonal vaginal steam once every three to four months, shortly before menstruation, to coincide with the change in the seasons. As one season ends and another begins, the solstices and equinoxes are the ideal times to rekindle your relationship with yourself.

• Cramps: The endometrial lining is loosened and the pelvic muscles are soothed and relaxed by the herbal steam. One cause for why yoni steams are particularly beneficial for endometriosis sufferers. One or two weeks before to menstruation, women who have pain, bloating, or tiredness during their periods should steam once a week to help the uterine lining shed. Once your period starts, you'll probably notice a shift in the fluid you pass. After your cycle is finished, you can steam once to remove any extra materials.

•For fertility: You can yoni steam from the pre-ovulation stage till ovulation if you're actively trying to get pregnant. Yoni steam may assist to improve the environment for conception by moistening uterine membranes, making them more responsive. For the purpose of ensuring that the tissue is moist and that the cervical fluids are clean and plentiful, women who are having trouble getting pregnant should steam once a week and twice during pre-ovulation. Prior to seeing results, plan on steaming for at least three months. If you suspect you could be pregnant or after possible pregnancy, avoid steaming.

•After a miscarriage: Having a healing experience that pampers your body and womb is crucial to complete healing. Miscarriage is a serious deal. A lovely method to nurture your body and emotions is to create a yoni steam ritual. Once the bleeding has stopped, it is best to prepare your yoni steam.

• Postpartum: Yoni steams help the body shed fluids, provide nourishing heat, and speed the womb's return to its pre-pregnancy size. Herbal postpartum steams aid in the removal of the entire body's birth fluids. Within the first nine days following delivery, postpartum mothers are advised to take steams by Mayan midwives. Within the first nine days following delivery, a healthy mother who gave birth naturally will experience three steams. The number 9 is a spiritual tradition used by Maya midwives. During the first nine days after giving birth, women often steam their vagina three times to promote healing and vaginal and uterine toning.

I also provided yoni steams for women who had caesarian deliveries in my practice. I was directly caring for the mother during the steam in these circumstances. The new mother shouldn't try to do the steams by themselves or unattended during the first few days after giving birth.

• Yoni steam can provide emotional support and regenerate vaginal tissue during peri-, meno-, and post-menopausal stages. It can also hydrate dry vaginal tissue. In the first few years of menopause, a few yoni steams are advised for those going through the process to make sure the uterine membrane is extremely clean when it stops menstruating. Even a year after the last menstrual period, some menopausal women report passing clots and dark, thick blood.

•Following a hysterectomy, warmth and heat are calming therapies for scar tissue and can be a wonderful way to reclaim your femininity.

• A yoni steam can be a gentle approach to rehabilitate after a sexual trauma or any time your body feels violated. The yoni steam gives you some peace and quiet so you can meditate, love your body, and feel cared for.

•following a divorce or separation A yoni steam is a lovely method to end and purify that chapter of your life if you are no longer with your sexual partner and feel the need to release the old or poisonous energy that doesn't serve you.

What time of day is ideal for a yoni steam?

Generally speaking, as long as you are not menstruation, you can steam at any time of the month. It is preferable to take a steam later in the evening so that you can quickly get into bed thereafter.

When is a yoni steam inappropriate?

Yoni steams should not constantly be used! There are times in our lives and reasons why we shouldn't take the steam. If you are: Do not perform a yoni steam.

• Avoid steaming when ovulating if you're trying to get pregnant.

• If you are expecting or suspect that you are expecting

• If you have an intrauterine device (IUD), you may only do so for 5 to 10 minutes, according to some

- Be suffering from a fever and an active internal illness (cervical, uterine, or ovarian inflammation).

- Do you have any open herpes sores or blisters? If so, soak the diseased region until the blisters have healed.

- Menstruating

The ideal herbs for yoni steams

Similar to getting a facial for your uterus, a yoni steam is comparable to steam washing the uterine wall. Choose herbs that are mild enough for your tongue and eyes.

- Lavender is a fragrant herb with antiseptic and antibacterial characteristics that are calming and effective in cleansing the vaginal area.

- Rosemary aids in the circulation of blood and old fluids while acting as an antibacterial. It stimulates and purifies the yoni and helps you retrieve or remember lost facets of who you are.

•Lemon balm is a fragrant herb with antiviral properties that also relieves itching.

•Dandelion promotes reproductive and endocrine health. It assists the body's elimination of extra estrogen, carbohydrates, and poisons.

• The golden-yellow blooms of the calendula plant are antibacterial and soothing to injured tissues. Additionally, it helps treat and relieve heaviness and cramping.

•The yoni is energized, stimulated, and restored by peppermint.

•The grandmother of all herbs is chamomile. It aids in easing pain, stress, and cramping. It smells wonderful.

• Yarrow is an effective anti-infection agent and works wonders on sore, bruised, and patched tissues.

• Uva Ursi is a herb that alkalinizes the body and is especially effective for UTI and reproductive infections.

Supporting plants for the reproductive and urinary systems

Motherwort, Peony, Damiana, Oregano, Basil, Raspberry Leaf

Tonifying, tightening, and drying herbs:

Rose, Yarrow, Witch Hazel, and Juniper

Herbs that moisturize and calm:

For their mucilaginous properties, which can help with softening and cleansing as well as their high mineral content, comfrey, marshmallow, plantain, and seaweeds like kombu and bladderwrack are all added. Yoni steams can provide your pelvis with profound healing, moisturizing, and warmth.

Setting out for Yoni Steam

The first time you set something up, it seems like a lot of work! Once you've set it up a few times, you'll realize how simple it is. The bathroom, your bedroom, or meditation rooms are all good places to set up. You might want to gaze at an altar or out a window. Put your steam bowl in a location where you have space and can sit comfortably. If you want to keep warm, make sure to put the chair on carpet or wear socks.

• Set a saucepan with a lid and 3–4 quarts of water on the stove to boil. Once the water is at a roaring boil, lower the heat, add one cup of tightly packed dry herbs and seaweed (or one quart of fresh herbs), and simmer for five to ten minutes. Turn off the heat, cover the pot, and steep for a further 10 minutes. The volatile oils in the herbs should stay in the steam and not escape.

• While waiting, gather a sheet, some towels, and a wool blanket to wrap around you. Once you're seated, they should be wrapped around you to create a sweat lodge-like structure for your lower body. Use pillows behind you and, if preferred, place towels on top of the seat.

• Move the herb pot under the chair's open seat when you're ready to sit and steam. Open the lid of the steam once you have seated yourself, made yourself comfortable, and draped yourself. Close the steam tent so that no cold air enters; otherwise, adjust to the heat and use the drape to allow in fresh air while you settle in. After that, relax in your yoni steam.

• Unwind, practice meditation, read something uplifting, listen to music, connect with your pelvis, womb, and vagina, and pay attention to what your body is trying to tell you.

The ideal steaming time is between 20 and 30 minutes. Be aware of your body. Continue as necessary. While utilizing the steams, pay particular attention to the week just before bleeding. Use caution if you are pregnant or bleeding. The best time to steam the uterus is right after childbirth and right after menopause.

What to anticipate following Yoni Steaming

You might feel incredibly calm, emotional, or exhausted right after steaming. After that, stay covered in sheets and spend the remainder of the evening in a comfortable bed. Your reproductive system will continue to benefit from the yoni bath herbs while you sleep, and you will awaken feeling pampered, cherished, and nurtured.

You might experience a variety of things in the days that follow, including changes in your cycle, a lighter period, the release of dark blood, clots, and increased feminine sensitivity. Changes could appear immediately or gradually.

It's a little alarming to discover that yoni steaming seems to be universally shunned by the medical establishment—not because it's harmful, but rather because it's a technique about which doctors are insufficiently informed. It begs the question of whether medical professionals are missing something if they dismiss this general health practice without considering any potential advantages. I think this is bad because it makes sense to attempt steaming with herbs and water before turning to the medical model if you are experiencing alarming symptoms. Yet when you discuss it, they portray it as absurd and harmful and recommend NSAIDs when, in the majority of cases, using steam is a perfectly healthy and logical method of taking care of yourself.

One thing I worry about with excessive yoni steaming is that it can mess with the flora and microbiome in your vaginal canal. Your vagina is totally capable of self-cleansing and typically doesn't require cleaning. Bacteria in a healthy vagina help maintain the proper vaginal pH, but altering this environment (via steaming, douching, etc.) might raise the risk of infection.

Another issue I have with the way Yoni steams are marketed is that they imply that you are unclean in some way, that your natural odor needs to be covered up, and that your discharge is disgusting. There are various products available that try to sell you expensive items that you don't actually need. Perpetuating the false notion that women, and particularly their genitalia, are filthy and require cleaning.

The dangers of vulvovaginal burns could increase with vaginal steaming.

Please be advised to seek care from a holistic care practitioner, such as a midwife, naturopath, herbalist, or acupuncturist, if you are experiencing recurrent infections or have concerns.

Yoni steams provide a chance for us to reconnect with our yoni/uterus after trauma, violation, abuse, surgery, or even just cultural alienation. Yoni steaming is a self-care technique that can be used to improve your health, balance your menstrual cycles, facilitate the passage through life's stages, reveal the secret power of your womb, and let go of toxic emotions like stress, tension, and stagnation.

The top beauty maxims every woman needs to know.

The internet is a wealth of knowledge when it comes to skin and hair care. Everybody has a unique perspective on everything. As a result, it might be difficult to determine which treatments and fashions are best for your skin. Because of this, we've compiled a list of the top tips for taking care of your skin and hair that every woman should be aware of.

Understand your skin and hair types.

The key is knowledge. Finding out what type of skin you have is the first thing you should do to keep yourself healthy. You can have combination skin, oily skin, acne-prone skin, or dry skin. Knowing your skin type makes it simpler to find the right solution for you. You can choose between having straight, curly, or wavy hair. It might be light, heavy, or dense. Each type of skin and hair requires a unique strategy for maintenance. Damage and additional issues may come from using the incorrect items or techniques.

The significance of hydration and moisture cannot be overstated.

No matter what kind of skin you have, you should always use a moisturizer. Now, depending on your skin's needs, the type of moisturizer you use may change. If you have dry skin, you might choose a cream that is thicker and more moisturizing. On the other hand, oily skin will need a light moisturizer that is non-comedogenic or water-based. While mild creams with few ingredients and no added scent are excellent for sensitive skin. When it comes to your hair, it is comparable. No matter what type of hair you have, it's critical to provide your hair with the hydration it needs following a wash. The use of conditioners, deep conditioners, and hair masks is quite helpful in repairing damage and maintaining the health of your hair.

Sun protection is more crucial than you would think.

Everyone is aware that they should use sunscreen throughout the summer and while they are outside, but they may not be aware that even indoors, their skin is still susceptible to the sun's UV radiation. Skin cancer, sunburns, dryness, rashes, spots, patches, and even accelerated aging are just a few of the issues that exposure to the sun can bring about. Therefore, even while you are inside, you should use sunscreen. It needs to be a consistent component of your morning skincare routine. The sun can be quite harmful to your hair as well. One method of UV protection for your hair is with sun-protective serums. You can also wear a cap or wrap your hair in a scarf to reduce the amount of time you are exposed.

Understanding what you put in your body

There is more information available to you now thanks to rising consumerism and awareness. Knowing what you are putting on your skin or hair is so crucial. Always read the product's ingredients label before using it. Never overlook performing a patch test to identify any ingredients that can trigger a reaction on your skin. The most essential thing to remember is to always consult a dermatologist if you have any questions about what is best for your skin or hair.

The interior influences the exterior.

No matter how carefully you take care of your skin, it won't matter if you do not take good care of your inside organs. Your skin and hair are directly impacted by what you eat and drink. It's crucial to get enough water in your system for both your physical and aesthetic wellbeing. Skin that is soft, elastic, and well-hydrated is more likely to have a well-hydrated body. Your skin and hair can benefit greatly from consuming a lot of nutrient-dense green leafy vegetables. A bright and healthy physique can be boosted by eating the proper amount of fruits and vegetables that are high in vitamins C and E.

Tips for maintaining good skin throughout the season

Don't believe the myth that caring for your skin in the heat is difficult. Due to the skincare issues that the wet season presents. While the rain offers relief from the intense heat, it also brings humidity and wetness, which can lead to a variety of skin problems like infections, allergies, and fungus.

We are sensitive to rashes, acne, and other skin disorders. How then, can you care for your skin in the wet season? You must realize that it is crucial to adjust your skincare routine in accordance with the changing seasons.

Ladies, implement this advice into your skincare routine.

Daily face washing

Dust, filth, and oil accumulate excessively during the wet season. As a result, washing your face is crucial. Try to wash your face three times a day if you can. By preventing fungal infections, you can fight oily skin and open pores.

Consistently exfoliate

Your skin can become a breeding ground for a variety of germs and bacteria during the rainy season, which can lead to severe acne and other skin problems. Exfoliate your skin with a gentle scrub to remove dead skin cells and clear clogged pores in order to avoid this issue.

Consistently moisturize

You may think you don't really need a moisturizer as the rainy season approaches due to the increased humidity. But because of the dryness brought on by this climate, you need to apply lotion to your skin. Additionally, having enough moisture will aid in wrinkle reduction and skin radiance maintenance.

Keep your skin hydrated

During the monsoon season, you tend to perspire a lot, which can leave your skin looking pale and dreary. The most crucial thing you can do to maintain healthy skin during this season is to stay hydrated. Throughout the day, drink enough water to stay hydrated and attain healthy-looking skin. Doing so can keep your skin clear of toxins, which can cause acne and pimples.

Take care of your lips

During the monsoon season, your skin is exposed to more humidity, which causes it to lose its capacity to absorb moisture and become dry and chapped. The weather also has an effect on your lips. Use a scrub on your lips to keep them smooth and get rid of chapped lips.

www.ingramcontent.com/pod-product-compliance
Lightning Source LLC
LaVergne TN
LVHW010555160826
845677LV00013B/3131

* 9 7 9 8 8 4 5 9 6 5 8 8 2 *